For Gay,
best,
Page Dickey
Erica Lennard

THANKS!
Peter Wheelwright

Breaking Ground

ARTISAN *New York*

Breaking Ground

PORTRAITS OF TEN GARDEN DESIGNERS

PAGE DICKEY   *Photographs by* ERICA LENNARD

DESIGNER: Jim Wageman
PRODUCTION DIRECTOR: Hope Koturo

Library of Congress Cataloging-in-Publication Data
Dickey, Page.
    Breaking ground : portraits of ten garden designers /
Page Dickey : photographs by Erica Lennard.
      p.   cm.
    Includes index.
    ISBN 1–885183–37-2
    1. Garden--Design 2. Landscape architecture.
3. Landscape architects—United States. 4. Landscape
architects—Europe. 5. Gardens—United States—
Pictorial works. 6. Gardens—Europe—Pictorial works.
I. Lennard, Erica.   II. Title.
SB472.45.D535   1997
712'.092'24—dc21   97-15288
                                          CIP

Published in 1997 by Artisan,
a division of Workman
Publishing Company, Inc.
708 Broadway
New York, NY 10003

Printed in Italy
10 9 8 7 6 5 4 3 2 1
First Printing

PAGE 1: *Old roof tiles were set in cement in a sunburst pattern by Alain Idoux for the ground beneath an arbor in Provence.* PAGES 2-3: *A pool of Astilbe chinensis 'Pumila' tints the ground beneath beech trees in a garden designed by Nancy McCabe in New York.* PAGES 6-7: *Goldfields and grasses form a soft sunlit carpet under oaks in a California garden created by Ron Lutsko.* PAGES 8-9: *Brilliantly colored, boldly textured plants that suit the climate of southern California are used in great sweeps by Nancy Power.* PAGE 10: *Glass kitchen doors open onto a dining terrace and a fountain fashioned from an old bronze urn by Madison Cox in New York City.*

FOR MY SISTER, ANNE WILSON
—PD

FOR DENIS COLOMB, WITH LOVE
—EL

Contents   *Dan* Pearson   *Nancy Goslee* Power

Steve Martino   Ron Lutsko   Nancy McCabe

Piet Oudolf   *Louis* Benech

Introduction

A NEW CONSCIOUSNESS HAS CREPT INTO the designing of gardens. Slowly, subtly, an awareness of our fragile environment, and a sensitivity to the natural landscape and its ecological limits, is coloring the creative process of building gardens. We are no longer making gardens in a void, but rather seeking to relate them to their surroundings.

This consciousness was the common thread that Erica Lennard and I discovered as we went around the United States and parts of Europe talking to garden designers and seeing their work. No matter where they were gardening, whether in the desert or on the northern coast of Maine, we sensed in them a deep concern, a passion, really, for the indigenous landscape, and a desire to relate their gardens to that landscape intellectually as well as visually.

At the same time, and seemingly quite apart from this vital sense of place and serious ecological commitment, Erica and I found a fresh, irreverent spirit among the designers. They had a willingness to stretch the rules, be experimental, have fun with the art form of gardening. They referred often to their favorites among the great garden makers of the twentieth century—Beatrix Farrand, Roberto Burle Marx, Dan Kiley, Thomas Church, Charles de Noailles, Christopher Lloyd, Nicole de Vesian—and felt their influence. In the same spirit of their mentors, they were not afraid to push the limits of design as we know it. A boldness and sense of humor ran through their work like a bright thread in a tapestry.

All the designers spoke of allowing a little wildness to enter their gardens. Nature was revered and permitted to muss things up a bit. Steve Martino talked fondly of letting his gardens go to wrack and ruin. Patrick Chassé liked his gardens to bleed imperceptibly into the natural scenery.

They all knew the value of boldness with color and shape, how the lavish use of a single plant, for example, creates a powerful visual effect. And they all sought for some meaning in their garden designs, something beyond practicality—a symbolic marriage with the landscape and the character of a given site, capturing the atmosphere of the place.

Over and over, I heard the words "simple" and "simplicity" from the designers. Each of them was striving to simplify, to learn restraint, in their choice of plants, in their use of color and line, and in the overall effect of their designs. Nancy McCabe spoke about restraint as the hardest thing to achieve in design.

The fact that there are only ten designers in the book has more do to with our desire to profile the designers in depth than with the availability of choices. And it is a mere coincidence that men outnumber women. In the best of all circumstances, more areas of the United States and more countries abroad would be represented than we had room for here. These ten men and women are simply our examples of a vibrant, exciting core group of artists who are bringing new dimensions to garden design.

A COLORIST IN THE ENGLISH GARDEN

Dan Pearson

Dan Pearson

*I*N A VIBRANT, YOUNG, ECLECTIC neighborhood of London, Dan Pearson lives in a top-floor flat opening onto a nine-by-twelve-foot section of rooftop. Here he has created a tiny whimsical garden among the chimney pots. But he designs larger gardens for clients all around London and the English countryside. What causes people to seek him out, what sets Dan apart as a designer, is the freshness of his work, its lighthearted originality. His gardens have a freedom about them, a joyful wildness and exuberant use of color, that perhaps has something to do with youthful irreverence.

Dan is in his early thirties, and does not seem bound by England's centuries-old garden traditions. He designs as though he were brushing aside the rules, going by his own instinct and his sense of what looks good or feels right in a specific setting. Formality and geometry are forsaken in favor of curves and waves of plantings that are allowed to go wildly to seed. Individual plants—perennials, herbs, and grasses—are massed in immodest numbers when he has the space, and then played against each other to achieve a certain "atmosphere." He has a passion for color ("Color always turns me on," he says) and a flair for using it in bold strokes and startling combinations. All of this artistry, however, is founded on a solid, no-nonsense knowledge of plants and gardening practices.

Dan has been gardening all his life. He was "hooked," he said, when his father made a pond for him when he was six years old. "Both my parents were

PRECEDING PAGES: *A path of crushed slate and cobblestone swirls past yellow and apricot foxtail lilies in an exuberant barnyard garden where Dan Pearson plays with waving grasses and sweeps of perennials in tones of orange, red, maroon, cream, and pale yellow. Color, motion, and atmosphere play important roles in his designs.* LEFT: *Dan allows a certain wildness to invade his gardens, achieving a style he calls "organized chaos." An explosion of oxeye daisies weaves through the entrance gate to Home Farm in Northamptonshire.*

artists. My father was a painter and my mother was a textile and fashion designer, so I grew up in an environment that was visually oriented. Everything was on a high aesthetic level. My mother and father loved to garden and they gave me a huge amount of room in which to experiment"—a thirty-by-three meter plot, to be exact, where Dan planted a yellow border. "It was purple and yellow, actually. I loved yellow. I would find plants and bring them home and the garden grew and grew and became my passion."

Besides his parents, two other people were pivotal in shaping Dan's gardening sensibility. One, a neighbor named Geraldine Noyes, had a garden along the lane where Dan lived as a boy. "It was a wild garden, really. She traveled a lot and collected seed, and then grew the plants on. She had a pond where I spent hours, just looking."

When Dan was ten, he started to go to a garden in the village that was open to the public, owned by a Mrs. Pumphrey. "She was a natural colorist and a fantastic horticulturalist. The garden was large and informal, with a stream set in rolling farmland. I used to visit every weekend, and, after a while, she offered me a job. Between the ages of twelve and sixteen, I gardened there with her every weekend. It was very influential."

By the time Dan was seventeen, gardening was second nature to him. But he wanted to learn more about plants from all over the world in order to acquire a solid technical background, which he felt was necessary if he wanted to design gardens. He considered landscape architecture school, but decided that it didn't offer enough horticulture. "I was so plant-led." If you don't know the repertoire, Dan suggests, how can you perform? So he tackled it from a different direction, and took courses, first at The Royal Horticultural Society Garden at Wisley, and then at The Edinburgh Botanic Garden. While at Edinburgh, he won a scholarship for study in Spain, where he fell in love with alpine meadows. It was the begining of many journeys to view new landscapes and learn about plants in for-

Daisies bloom wildly in front of the terrace wall at Home Farm. Above, foxgloves, alliums, lavender, purple fennel, and "black" opium poppies spill out of narrow borders to romp through the paving. White roses and the gray foliage of lamb's ears and artemisia complement the colors of purple, maroon, and lavender Dan favors here.

A romantic profusion of flowers greets the visitor to Home Farm in late May. Dan has an ongoing "love affair" with this garden which he continues to develop in collaboration with its owner, Frances Mossman, a textile designer.

eign countries. Dan was accepted by The Royal Botanic Gardens at Kew for further study, and took field trips to see the flora of the Himalayas and Israel.

It was with Frances Mossman, however, that Dan was able to find an expression for all his gardening inspiration and study. "I was seventeen when I was introduced to Frances. She was teaching textile design with my mother, and had a garden in London. She had been inspired by Beth Chatto, whose garden exhibits at Chelsea had an air of wildness that was revolutionary at the time, and she needed help. We met, hit it off, and we've been gardening together ever since."

In the late 1980s, Frances and her husband bought a farmhouse in Northamptonshire along with several acres of land. The stone and brick house backs up to a natural wood and has a view of gently rolling hills and pastures grazed by cows and sheep. Dan has been developing the garden there, in collaboration with Frances, since 1988. Both Dan and Frances say they are completely sympathetic with each other, and, although Frances is not knowledgeable about plants, as a textile designer she has a feeling for color combinations and patterns. She and Dan will discuss at length the color scheme for each part of the garden, then Dan will implement it. "At Kew," Dan says, "you consider the individual plant. But in the garden, it is the whole picture that counts. Like textile samples, gardens are always about combinations. What stimulates me is how you can combine plants to get certain effects."

Recently, Frances and her husband made an apartment in their barn for Dan, and he travels there often to stay a day or two and indulge what he calls "my absolute love affair with this garden." It is a long-range project that evolves and grows as Dan's style matures and becomes more confident. But the garden holds on to its atmosphere of romantic wildness and painterly richness that Dan established from the start.

As you approach Home Farm, you come to an iron gate, smothered in oxeye daisies, that leads through a stone retaining wall. Up a few steps, between box bushes and white roses that spill over the wall, is a paved terrace by the front door. More roses and clematis clamber up the house walls, and a discerning assortment of rare and common flowers, planted in the terrace beds, have seeded freely in the cracks of the paving. In June, foxgloves and white clover romp with purple fennel and opium poppies of a maroon so dark they are almost black. Fragrance is an obvious priority

here, and the choice of color combinations—white, gray, lavender, purple, and plum—is orchestrated to continue from spring until frost. There is a feeling of abandonment, of letting go, of allowing nature to continue painting the picture that Dan and Frances started. It is part of Dan's method and intention that this should happen. "I like to leave gardens to develop a certain wildness."

When the Mossmans bought their farmhouse, soil from the hill behind the house had washed down to such a degree that it covered the first-floor windows halfway up. Dan scooped out a small graveled terrace at the bottom of the hill, and then leveled the steep, south-facing land enough for narrow brick walks to circle up and around the slope. Here he made a larger, more dramatic garden. Against a backdrop of natural woodland, Dan planted dusky purple-leaved hazels, smokebush, and golden-variegated dogwoods. Then he planted perennials and herbs in vast sweeps, playing with a wide range of colors, from orange and purple to

magenta and pale yellow. At first, shrub roses and large silver-leaved plants like cardoons were added to the scheme for a bold, "gardenesque" effect. But recently, Dan and Frances decided they wanted the back garden to "feel more like a woodland glade," and Dan has now replaced one-third of the original plants, which he felt were too ornamental. All the roses have been removed, except for the plum-leaved species, *Rosa glauca,* which has a delicate wild look. In addition, all the statuesque silver-leaved plants have been discarded. In their place, Dan has planted a variety of grasses, knotweeds (*persicarias*), and thistles. More alliums have been added, and Joe-Pye weed, and his favorite buddleia, the very dark purple one called 'Black Knight.' Dan always uses lots of deep colors—plum, chocolate, burgundy, violet—that add shadow and drama to his color schemes. Near the top of the glade is a path that opens onto a tiny circular meadow where he naturalized daffodils, camassias, fritillarias, and orange dandelions in the grass.

LEFT: *An extravagant planting of shrubs and perennials fills the south-facing slope behind the house. Dan has recently replaced some of the more ornamental plants—like the silver-leaved cardoon—with grasses, knotweeds, thalictrums, and eupatoriums for a more naturalistic atmosphere.*

RIGHT: *A starry head of* Allium christophii *echoes the color of* Erysimum 'Bowles Mauve' *on the front terrace.*

LEFT: *Pale yellow* Phlomis russeliana *and purple sage are planted in bold masses with bright orange* Euphorbia griffithii *'Fireglow' on the bank behind Home Farm.*
RIGHT: *Chartreuse lady's mantle, tumbling along a path with deep magenta* Geranium psilostemon *and shaggy white astrantias, is set off by purple-leaved shrubs in the back garden.*

This back garden has a romantically extravagant atmosphere. Walking through it, you can lose yourself among the lush foliage of shrubs and flowers, absorbing their patterns and rich, saturated colors. From the house, the garden seems to hurtle down the bank and spill out onto the terrace. Seeding is encouraged here, too. In fact, Frances says, "We don't cut anything down; the seed heads are so nice to see in the fall." Before the replanting of the back garden, Frances said

there was not much to see in winter besides bare earth. The bold sweeps of ornamental grasses now extend visual interest into the winter months.

Until recently, no evergreens, besides the box bushes at the front gate, were used at Home Farm to color the winter landscape. Dan's gardens tend to be primarily herbaceous, with few bones other than the woody branches of deciduous shrubs. But his newest garden project at the Mossmans' is different. In the

field between the house and the barn, Dan established an L-shaped line of young lime trees, connecting the two buildings and creating a courtyard. Within this new square, he planted "huge, static yews, clipped into amorphous shapes," along with pruned mounds of rue, underplanting them with grasses—the tall, graceful stipa and the shorter molinia. "I wanted the grasses to echo the adjacent fields, and the rue and yews to seem like emerging hills." Sea lavender, "Miss Wilmott's ghost" (that silvery thistle, *Eryngium giganteum*), and blue flax were added to appear "like wild flowers you might find in a field." It is a garden to be looked at mostly from a distance, Dan says, as you approach Home Farm, or as you stand by the front door. It was made to express an atmosphere, always Dan's priority,

using plants that have the mood, the feel, of the surrounding landscape. With its strong structure, it should look as good in winter as it does in summer.

Grasses are a new enthusiasm of Dan's. He loves their movement, their silhouettes and parchment-like colors, and they play a major role now in all his gardens. A walled area behind the barn at the Mossmans' is the site of a newly developed red garden, where grasses are used as a foil to complement the fiery hues of poppies, torch lilies, cannas, and crocosmias. Although the perimeter of the red garden is rectangular, bound by the barn and its stone walls, Dan has created swirling paths around a central bed he describes as being shaped like a cobble. The paths are actually fashioned out of some rippled cobblestone and crushed

sort against another in long overlapping waves with striking results.

Although beautifully drawn planting schemes were made for Frances of each garden area, Dan drew them up after the fact. He paints with plants as on a canvas, then records the results. But nature is always allowed a hand in a garden's development, and Dan is always editing and improving, so it soon diverges from its form on paper.

Dan planted a young wood of native trees for the Mossmans' five-year-old son, with the idea that the trees and the boy might grow up together. He also described a garden he made for a four-year-old child in Norwich. Keeping in mind how the garden would look from a child's-eye view, Dan built an enormous wigwam out of chestnut posts tied together with string. String ropes hung from its sides for vines (and the child) to climb. Dan carved a hole in a hedge and made a "cave entrance" out of wattle. He also created a meadow with

ABOVE: Glass beads dangle from the doorway opening onto Dan's rooftop. The doorway juts out from the roof like a dormer and is topped by a giant nest of twigs holding a topiary bird. **RIGHT** *and* **FAR RIGHT**: *Airy, moving plants like stipa, Dan's favorite orna-* *mental grass, and* Verbena bonariensis *are planted in tall galvanized containers to wave against the chimney pots of London. Fragrant white daturas nod in a corner of Dan's garden where every foot of roof space is bursting with flowers and grasses.*

slate he discovered when he dug down through several feet of old cow manure behind the barn. The plant list for this small garden is extraordinarily rich and varied, and yet Dan managed to plant a number of them in great swaths. Frances is proud of a gorgeous red potentilla she had found for the garden. "Dan said it was just what he would have picked. But I would have bought only a few. Dan bought a few hundred!" It is Dan's style to use single plants in bold numbers, playing one paths. "Imagine running through grasses as tall as you are!" He planted a circle of silver birches to be an enclosure just for the child. "It wasn't sentimental," Dan said. He merely fashioned a fantasy out of nature.

Dan's own garden is another sort of fantasy, an "unnatural" one. A rooftop garden is very different from a garden in the country, where the surrounding landscape influences your design, Dan explains. "It is totally artificial." Because everything is in pots or tubs, nature cannot have a hand in the garden's development. "It is all a fake." When plants become exhausted, the only recourse is to throw them out. On the other hand, Dan says, "it's nice to play around with things." Indeed, Dan obviously has fun on his rooftop doing just that. It is a tiny space with a view of chimney pots and, in the distance, the Houses of Parliament. A small cafe table and chair take up the center space and are surrounded by an explosion of dancing, waving flowers and grasses. Large galvanized metal containers (the kind you see in florist's shops), planted with tall grasses and fragrant herbs, line a shelf along the perimeter of the terrace, their contents waving airily with the slightest breeze. Every bit of space is used for growing things—annuals, shrubs, perennials—clustered in tubs or lined up in rows of small tin buckets. Purple morning glories climb latticework attached to the slanted roof, and on top of a dormer, a topiary bird rests on a giant nest of twigs. In one corner, Dan has enclosed a curved wooden bench with tall willow canes woven together and decorated with glass beads. A sense of fun emanates from this garden, a playfulness that makes you smile and feel good. And yet even here, Dan's combinations of plants would impress the most jaded, sophisticated plantsman.

"I don't do rooftops for clients," Dan says emphatically. They are "alien enviroments" in which you have to deal with elements in extremes—intense light, desiccating wind. Having responsibility for any rooftop but your own can become "a nightmare." But

Dan did design a gold medal-winning "London Roof Garden for the Nineties" at the 1996 Chelsea Flower Show. Using plants—many of them Mediterranean herbs—that he knew could stand up to the rigors of a rooftop, he created a boldly textured garden in a subdued color scheme of beiges, browns, silvers, and greens. "I was interested in just barely suggesting a color." Decking of natural wood and a floor of oatmeal-hued pebbles flowed out from the house and into the garden. But Dan placed two brightly hued lounge chairs on the deck, and clustered red glasses on a table to "add a touch of electricity."

The curvaceous chairs, harking back to the 1950s, were designed by Dan and his brother, Luke, a furniture designer. "I said to Luke, I wanted something good in

the wind, voluptuous, and brightly colored." They found the perfect material in a nylon fabric used by the military to lift disabled people out of the water. This they slipped onto tubular frames shaped in an elongated S-curve. Dan enjoys working in collaboration with architects and artists on some of his projects. But, in defense of his own expertise, he says, "Gardening is a very dynamic medium. I don't know why it's not compared more frequently to other artistic disciplines like sculpture and architecture." Perhaps because, unlike a sculpture or a building, a garden is transitory and ephemeral.

Dan believes he is growing as a designer, feeling more confident, "reaching another level. I am becoming more of a purist, learning restraint." He works on a bigger scale now, and does more hardscaping (using hard materials, such as stone and brick, to create paths, walls and so on), with lines as well as curves, but his new planting is all naturalistic, using a lot of grasses. He is much influenced by German gardens, and the gardens of Oehme and van Sweden in America, but feels his own style is freer and wilder.

Dan often speaks of his compatriot Christopher Lloyd as an inspiration and of Great Dixter as his favorite garden. "It will always be worth looking at," he says. Even though an age gap of several decades separates Dan and Mr. Lloyd, they have a similar spirit and style in gardening. They both love bold color combinations, and they are not afraid of experimenting with plants, accepting and learning from the inevitable failures. It excites them to try out new ground, stretch the rules, design with a sense of adventure and fun. Of Lloyd's garden, Dan says, "It is so kooky, and it looks lived-in. He's having such a good time." You could say that Dan is having a good time too.

BOLD DESIGN IN THE SOUTHERN CALIFORNIA GARDEN

Nancy Goslee Power

Nancy Goslee Power

NANCY POWER RADIATES VITALITY. Architectural writer Michael Webb once likened meeting her to "opening the door to a warm gale," and, indeed, her personality envelopes you instantly in a glow of enthusiasm. As you walk into her design studio, you are struck by the countless small expressions of her spiritedness, and you are tempted to linger there to drink it all in. Dried leaves, cones, berries, and pods are carefully arranged in flat baskets on her work table, treasures that caught her eye or booty from garden visits around the mountains, canyons, and coastline of southern California. Maple leaves in hues of orange, yellow, and scarlet (colors

often seen in Nancy's gardens) are scattered on another tray, sent from a friend back east who knew she would thrill to these tokens of a New England autumn. A branch of tree banksia with huge exotic flower cones stands in a corner in a large tin jug. A topographical map of California, bumpy with mountains, fills one whole wall by the stairs. Nancy's own watercolors—views of gardens mostly, done for pleasure—line the other walls along with design sketches and plans of landscapes in various stages of development. Photographs, postcards—of an Italian garden, perhaps—and pieces of interesting designs torn out of magazines are tacked up as reminders of images she loves. Books are everywhere, on shelves, piled on tables, or in stacks on the floor by a comfortable sofa, offering information on every conceivable facet of design, indoors and out. Pieces of bark, pebbles, tiles, and architectural remnants are arranged as pleasing still lifes, but they are also there to be picked up and handled by clients or visitors.

PRECEDING PAGES: *Curving paths reveal unexpected vistas in a spectacular canyon garden above Los Angeles—the result of a collaboration between garden designer Nancy Power and architect owner, Richard Martin. Bold sculptural forms, like the dragon trees* (Dracaena draco) *in this view, and fluid*

sweeps of plants in striking colors are typical of Nancy's work. ABOVE: *Nancy's watercolors of gardens are pinned to the wall in her studio where dried flowers, leaves, and berries are arranged on tables and in vases—booty brought home from her travels.*
RIGHT: *The orange flowers of bird-of-paradise* (Strelitzia reginae), *the official flower of Los Angeles, dance above the writhing stalks of* Aloe arborescens *in the Martin garden.*

It is not a surprise to learn that Nancy worked as an interior designer before launching her gardening career. Her eye for composition, her love of color, and her skill in using it translate easily from one discipline to the other. Nancy's gardens vary wildly from small and intimate spaces to large architectural settings. But always you notice a lavish use of of color, bold and warm like Nancy herself—flowers in oranges, reds, and purples, glazed tiles in brilliant blue or green. "Tiles were flowers in Spanish gardens," she says, speaking of the California garden heritage from which she draws inspiration. Even the foliage she uses is strikingly colored: deep bronze and mahogany, felt grays, satin blues. Her plants are often employed as sculpture, played against each other and against the walls that inevitably enclose some part of her gardens.

Nancy says she doesn't feel she's in a garden unless it's enclosed, and certainly there is a historic precedent in southern California for walled courtyard gardens. The tradition goes back to the settlements of the Spanish missionaries in the late eighteenth and early nineteenth centuries. Their mission gardens incorporated walled orchards and vineyards, and always included an enclosed patio surrounding a fountain. In the first decades of this century, the concept of an enclosed garden was glorified in the great Italianate gardens being built in California, where series of terraces, or rooms, were made with walls and clipped hedges, framing vistas that captured the spectacular local scenery of mountains and ocean.

Italy and Italian gardens have influenced Nancy since she lived there as a young art student, as they influenced the work of those early twentieth century garden designers in California. She speaks admiringly of Lockwood de Forest as "one of the most visionary" of these golden-age designers and as an inspiration for her. His gardens were classically formal in structure and at the same time offbeat, including unconventional details such as a pattern of immense columns that hold nothing up, or unusual plants used in painterly combinations. He was brilliant at siting his gardens, typically focusing "on the splendor of the setting, call-

LEFT: *Nancy loves the look of the bronze-leaved phormiums she planted against the corrugated metal wall of Frank Gehry's startlingly unconventional home in Santa Monica.* RIGHT: *When Gehry asked Nancy to devise a planting scheme for the front of the house, it was completely exposed to the road. With agaves, leonotis, bird-of-paradise, the hollywood juniper, and a flaxleaf paper-bark tree, she screened the house and created privacy for a small courtyard behind the white stucco wall.*

ing attention to its stunning views and inviting them into his landscape." His own small garden in Santa Barbara, Nancy feels, shows a masterly use of space. Working outward from his small Romanesque villa, he created a feeling of intimacy in a series of outdoor rooms designed to be lived in. At the same time, he extended the garden by framing with trees a "borrowed" view of a distant mountain.

In her book *The Gardens of California,* Nancy describes her home ground as an "eclectic paradise" made up of a variety of people so "noisy with ideas and perspectives" that their gardens are inevitably going to be wildly disparate. "But," she writes, "if there is one aspect linking all our gardens here, perhaps it is an appreciation of the majesty of our surroundings, and a desire to get outside and live our lives in the sunshine." Her own designs for gardens, whether large and sweeping or sheltered and intimate, always have this in mind.

"My best jobs play off architecture," Nancy says, and she has had the good fortune to work with some visionaries in the field. The architect Frank Gehry, a

filled it with agaves, aloes, bird-of-paradise, and leonotis
—"old L.A. plants from the twenties." The plants serve
as a lush screen between the sidewalk and a small front
terrace, at the same time contrasting handsomely with
the mustard clapboard and silvery metal walls of the
house in the background. As you turn the corner of the
sidewalk, you come upon a a stunning row of sword-
like bronze-leaved phormiums, which Nancy enjoyed
playing against the corrugated siding of a galvanized
metal wall.

In suburban Brentwood, Nancy landscaped another
project of Gehry's, a residential complex of buildings
designed for Maria Schnabel and her husband. A series
of startling, powerful one-room pavilions are arranged
like a bizarre village within a walled enclosure. Nancy's
challenge was to create a landscape strong enough to
stand up to the visual power of these structures and
help tie them together. Her favored palette of purple,
red, brilliant orange, gray-green, and bronze seemed
appropriate against the silver, burnished copper, and
stark white of the modern facades. Strap-leaved plants
such as birds of paradise and bronze flaxes were used
in profusion. Squat palms and statuesque cannas add
their own dramatic silhouettes. A grove of olive trees at
one end of the complex is underplanted with gray Mexican grasses studded with orange California poppies.
Even on the sidewalk outside the complex, where
glimpses of Gehry's towers and copper dome merely
hint at the Oz-like land within the stucco walls, Nancy's
otherworldly planting of blue-green agaves writhing in
a sea of fleshy senecio extends the visual fantasy.

In another part of Brentwood, high up on a hillside above Los Angeles, Nancy collaborated with the
architect Richard Martin to create a fantastic garden
surrounding his house. Nancy speaks of that three-year
collaboration as "an experience of constant challenge,
discovery, and surprise." "Dick pushed me to go that
step beyond," she says when explaining how she decided upon the bold masses of textured plants that swim

neighbor of Nancy's in Santa Monica, has turned to
Nancy more than once to compose a landscape of trees
and plants that will complement the outrageously dramatic sculptural elements of his designs. "You can't put
little roses" around one of Gehry's buildings, Nancy
remarked, amused at the mere thought of such incon-
gruity. Instead, she finds startlingly bold plants, some
native, others tropical or Mediterranean, to use as sympathetic compositions and backdrops.

Gehry's own house, a stucco bungalow that he
transformed with an extension of chain link, plywood,
and corrugated metal to the astonishment of his neighbors, sits cheek by jowl with other houses on a suburban street in Santa Monica. The house was "totally
exposed to the street" when Gehry called Nancy in to
design a front courtyard that would afford him some
privacy. She simply widened a low stucco wall around
the perimeter of the front yard to create a planter, and

together in vast waves of pattern and color. "Nothing would have to flower," she added, to achieve drama in this layered landscape. But flower they do—spikes of purple echiums and lavender, feathery buff and red grass plumes, and fleshy pink proteas. Nancy likens the landscape to an abstract painting, with its progressions of color from one plant grouping to another. "Planting one material in a mass is always a strong design," she says, pointing to whole sections of hillside that are blanketed with just one kind of perennial. Nancy had planted "an orchard" of wavy-branched olive trees on one part of the slope just below the house, and then underplanted it with a rich, ravishing carpet of blue-flowering prostrate rosemary, the dark rosemary dramatically pointing up the olives' ghostly pale trunks. In a lower part of the garden, a great solitary sweep of feather-headed grasses mimics the hairy trunks of a grouping of eucalyptus trees beyond it. Squat blue

palms rise from a virtual field of lavender falling down another part of the slope. Streams of purple iris lap the edges of a narrow curving path where tall cypresses capture a view of misted blue hills. "A garden should always feel voluptuous," Nancy declared—and this is an atmosphere she invariably achieves with her boldly generous, curvaceous plantings.

The designs of Roberto Burle Marx come to mind when viewing this garden, with its similar curvilinear style, exuberant color, and flowing masses of single plants. Burle Marx likened his first attempts at making

TOP LEFT: *Narrow paths cut through luxurious swaths of plants, like the echiums and lavender seen here in Richard Martin's garden.* BOTTOM LEFT: *A watercolor rendition by Nancy.* RIGHT: *A carpet of prostrate rosemary tumbles down a bank of olive trees just below Martin's house. A cypress divides a path and punctuates a view of the distant city.*

gardens to making a salad, but he then learned that less is more. His gardens were often like large-scale paintings formed of clean colorful shapes and flowing abstract forms that patterned themselves on the surrounding landscape.

Nancy is much moved by the artistry of Burle Marx, although she wasn't familiar with his work until she visited him on a trip to Brazil after the Martin garden was finished. She cites one difference in their styles: Burle Marx's landscapes, she believes, are meant to be viewed—"You don't 'hang' in his gardens, whereas my

gardens always have a place to go, to stop and rest." Indeed, chairs are clustered under a grove of blue gum trees in a secluded but central part of the Martin garden, and the terraces that wrap around the house offer numerous perches and seats for resting.

Martin designed his low-slung contemporary house to jut out from the top of the hillside, affording spectacular views on all sides. The walls, paths, and steps that extend from the house and wind down and around the steep site were also of his design. The house was painted a pink color Nancy describes as "pale

Roman red with coral and raspberry undertones," and this color to a great extent determined the garden's palette. A large enclosed courtyard near the entrance to the house, with a fountain and tables and chairs for entertaining, serves as a splendid setting for some particularly architectural plants juxtaposed against the pink of Martin's walls. Aloes sprout strange flowered stalks, narrow yellow-green cactus explode out of feathery gray artemisia, and a shaggy dragon tree (*Dracaena draco*) boldly defines a corner. Another dragon tree, a dramatic mop head of green fronds on a fat pearl-gray trunk, stands just outside the pink entry wall, silhouetted against the smoky panorama of the surrounding mountains.

Nancy stresses the importance of going out and "feeling the site" when designing a garden. She says she is obsessed with knitting together the outside and inside of a residence, "really working with that transition space, getting the garden to fit the house." She meets this challenge in an intimate space as well as she does in the vast openness of the Martin property.

Susan Stringfellow asked Nancy to devise a landscape for her small suburban plot in Brentwood that would connect a contemporary addition to her Spanish Colonial Revival house with the main structure. The simple, clean-lined architecture of the new wing repeated the materials of the original house, and Nancy's goal was to do the same with the garden, blending old established elements with new ones and linking the garden to the house "as a single harmonious composition, with little distinction between inside and out." The glass walls and unadorned French doors of the Stringfellows' dining room frame the small, colorful garden in a way that seems to bring it indoors. A stone terrace just outside the doors is shaded by a gnarled old pomegranate tree beyond which Nancy planted a sea of lavender. The lavender (*Lavandula multifida*), threaded with narrow curving paths of decomposed granite, stretches back to a border of

ABOVE: *In a small suburban garden in Brentwood, a walled front courtyard with a tiled fountain glimmers with wands of bright orange orchids* (Epidendrum), *planted all around its edges.* RIGHT: *A narrow water-lily pool, just outside a new contemporary bedroom wing of the Brentwood house, extends out into the back garden. Here, a sea of pungent Lavender multifida meets purple-flowering jacaranda trees and white banksia roses by the garage.*

Mediterranean plants, where purple-spiked echiums echo the lavender's flowering on a bigger, more dramatic scale. Brilliant purple-flowering jacaranda trees are planted in a tiny patch of grass meadow at the back of the property. To one side of the terrace, a long and narrow water-lily pool, extending the spare geometry of the new bedroom wing, further draws the house out into the garden.

Up in the Hollywood hills, Nancy worked over a period of years on a small enclosed garden for Claudia Weil and her husband, Walter Teller. The garden developed gradually from the steps of their glorified ranch house, down a slope clothed with an explosion of flowers, to a stunning swimming pool Nancy designed along the back wall of the property. It is a garden filled with a riot of color. "Not safe colors, either," Nancy is

quick to say. "Don't be afraid of color," she always advises, and her shameless combinations of pure brilliant hues here are a testament to her conviction.

In the warmth of the fall, red and orange bougainvillea spill down around the arched French doors on the garden side of the house. Felted stalks of yellow-flowering phlomis and wavy purple spires of Mexican sage ("used ad nauseum around here, but I don't mind ad nauseum") brush against the legs of anyone descending the garden steps to the pool area. Here, a perimeter wall painted a rich, tawny yellow and laced with delicate vines becomes a stunning backdrop for a lush border of patterned bronze and blue-green foliage. Burnished red pennisetums billow along the stone edging of the pool.

"When people ask me for an English border" (and easterners are apt to do this when they settle out west), "I think what they really mean is overblown," Nancy says wryly. Her garden borders are often spontaneously, merrily overblown, but they are certainly not English. They are always suited to their locality, made up of native Californian, Mexican, and Mediterranean plants. Suitability is important to Nancy, both in the choice of plants and the design of the garden. Because most of her clients have urban or suburban properties, she adheres inevitably and naturally to a Mediterranean style of garden, creating outdoor living spaces that feature enclosed patios, decoratively contained water, and dazzling color. "White gardens are difficult in California," she says. The color white tends to disappear. "A splash of red, on the other hand, can bring life to a composition—something I learned in decorating."

I asked Nancy how she approaches new commissions. Clients come to the office first, she said, to meet with her and "see if we jell." If they do, Nancy next meets the client at the site. Later, she returns to the site by herself "to study it quietly and write down all my thoughts." Then she goes back to her office and talks with her staff of young horticultural assistants and

LEFT: *Wood-framed glass doors from the dining room of the Brentwood house lead out onto a stone terrace half-shaded by an old pomegranate tree.* ABOVE: *On a property in the Hollywood hills, Nancy played with the textures and* foliage colors of bronze aeoniums, agaves, and echiums against a soft mustard yellow wall that borders the swimming pool. BELOW: *Yellow phlomis and pink-flowering aloes seem to explode from a ground cover of cerastium.*

architects about the project. At this point, with the help of a survey, they begin to devise a site plan. "The way I work," Nancy says, "is very collaborative. It's never 'I,' it's always 'we.'" Nancy suggests that her contribution to the team consists of the overview and the experience. It is obvious that she also offers her own special genius, her flair for designing with boldness and vivacity, exemplified by the spirited masses of colorful plants flourishing even in confined spaces.

Nancy recently recalled a memorable sight on the road to Santa Barbara. As she was driving along, she spotted a large, curious patch of orange in the distance but couldn't make out what it was until she got closer. "It was a whole field of marigolds," she said in astonishment and delight. "Of course, a whole field of anything can be fabulous," she admitted. "But I would rather see a field of marigolds with its exuberance and vulgarity —so sensual!—than one little precious darling of a plant that nobody has." The commonness of a plant never bothers Nancy. "The garden won't let you be too snooty," she says. "It puts you in your place all the time."

Feeling the excitement of life, "never letting your attitude become jaded"—that's the key thing, Nancy is certain, that makes the difference in design.

Large clumps of kangaroo-paw (Anigozanthos) *and the burnished red fountain grass,* Pennisetum setaceum *'Rubrum,' bloom by the pool Nancy designed in the Hollywood hills. Pale yellow* Phlomis russeliana *and coral pink* Aloe striata *pick up the color in the foreground.*

Madison Cox

*Madison*Cox

MADISON COX FELL IN LOVE in the 1980s with the Mogul gardens of Kashmir. They combine the sense of order and geometry that is so important to him with a feeling of lightheartedness and intimacy. "Unlike the great French gardens," he says, "they are not meant to impress you, to overpower you, but rather to draw you in." Visitors today take delight in the gardens in the same manner as their original owners did, sitting on rugs, picnicking, enjoying the shade and the murmuring of water and the fragrance of the flowers. The main design feature of Islamic gardens is the water that comes down a central canal, dividing beds dotted with flowers (for color and fragrance) and fruit trees (for shade). "Always," Madison explains, "there is this play of light and shadow and water, the sound of water. And there is, typically, a fanciful use of color. The Mogul gardens never seem stiff and rigid—they are sensual, they are about the idea of pleasure." They are meant as retreats, as places to escape the heat of India. "Imagine cool oases in a hot country —a great luxury."

Madison finds similarities between these Indian gardens and some gardens in France and Italy that have especially influenced him. The garden of Villa Lante, for instance, north of Rome, is one he finds enchanting for many of the same reasons. The main axis of this relatively small Renaissance garden is water. It starts as a stream from a natural spring in a half-wild woodland at the top of the garden and descends through channels and fountains to a four-sided pool surrounded by green parterres at the bottom. "As you follow the steps down the terraced hillside, you are accompanied by the sensual sound of water,

PRECEDING PAGES: *On a terrace overlooking the East River in New York City, Madison Cox planted large wooden Versailles boxes with crab apple trees to create a summer refuge.* **BELOW:** *A pool in a Long Island garden shows the influence of Indian design in Madison's work.* **RIGHT:** *Madison likes it best when a certain wildness softens the formal structure of his gardens. Behind a Greenwich Village brownstone, he decorated the walled perimeters of a long narrow garden with a series of old wooden columns, romantically entwined with*

ivy and Virginia creeper. Gravel paths surround a center bed of ivy underplanted with 'Tete-a-Tete' daffodils that is dominated by a majestic sycamore.

and again, there is this sense of pleasure, of refuge," Madison says.

The same holds true for another of his favorite gardens, Villa Noailles, created after World War II with extraordinary style and charm by the Vicomte de Noailles on a hillside near Grasse, in France. In this very personal, small-scale Italianate garden, sculptured hedges enclose intimate rooms and frame views of the distant valley, creating a sense of surprise and delight at each turn. Seats and statues and potted plants are placed with pure artistry to catch and please the eye and encourage lingering; water, with its trickling and splashing, also plays a vital role in the garden's atmosphere. The terraced site of the garden has a natural water source from springs that the Vicomte redirected into rills and canals. "At one point, a narrow rill of water runs down the middle of a small flight of stone steps," Madison says. "It is little things like this that make it such a magical garden. It is so very simple, and yet evocative of grander things."

Madison first visited the villa in the late 1970s before its creator, Charles de Noailles, died. "The wonderful thing was that when he was alive, the doors were always open to the public. This garden world is so generous," Madison notes. "That's what I love about it. If you called someone and said, 'You have such a marvelous collection of silver. May I come see it?' the person would hang up. Not true with gardeners."

Madison has lived abroad for much of his life and traveled extensively, absorbing different cultures and styles of design. His father was a ship captain, so Madison came by his traveling instinct naturally. His grandmother was an interior decorator, and her books on design filled their house when he was growing up. At age eighteen, Madison went to Paris to learn French and then go to design school. He studied drawing at an atelier, put together a portfolio, then applied and was accepted into a three-year enviromental design course at the Paris branch of the Parsons School of Design.

The course was "a hodgepodge of architecture, landscape, and interior design" taught by professors from all over Europe. The students themselves were a mixture of Americans, Europeans, and Arabs. "It was so eclectic, so interesting. In retrospect, I loved it." After he finished at Parsons, he worked for a year with an estate gardener in Normandy, getting a very practical education. "Real how-to stuff—you know, 'This is the way you clip roses,' etc. I worked on two gardens in Normandy and it was really wonderful." Then a friend asked Madison to help her out with a garden in Paris, and "one thing led to another."

In 1988, Madison returned from France to open his own design office in New York City. Perhaps his travels and his years living in a city have caused Madison to think of a garden foremost as a place of refuge. What more appropriate definition could there be for a garden in the frenzied city of New York? Here Madison transforms back lots, rooftops, and terraces into miniature paradises.

Madison's designs readily show his affinity for French, Italian, and Persian gardens, with their classical geometric symmetry. "I always start a project with a T square," he says, smiling. "The few times I've tried to do something wild, it was a total disaster. I like structure best." Madison thinks first about spacial balance—about the axial paths and views, the verticals and the water features, and shadow and light. "Then I like to break down the geometry with plants." He uses a simple palette of trees, vines, evergreen shrubs, and ground covers to dress and soften his structures. What results is invariably a spare, elegant, serene garden with a slight air of romance.

Madison professes to be no plantsman, though he admits he's becoming more interested in individual plants as he gets older. "During all those years living in France, I learned to appreciate a more minimal approach to planting." Simplified gardens, Madison feels, give a greater sense of peace, so essential in a refuge.

The columns in this Greenwich Village garden create alcoves where wooden seats and chaises offer respite from the summer heat. Madison latticed the walls between the columns, then encouraged vines to give the garden an air of abandonment.

Behind a brownstone in the Greenwich Village area of New York City, Madison recently created a romantic retreat for the composer and musician Jonathan Sheffer. The site is a typically long, narrow plot dominated by an ancient sycamore, which rises four stories from the ground and spreads its limbs across the garden. From the kitchen, at ground level, French doors open out onto a terrace where a dining table and chairs are sur-rounded by low planters filled with hostas and ivy. On the stuccoed wall that divides this area from the rest of the garden, an old bronze urn filled with water drips into a small semi-circular pool below it. Steps lead up to the main part of the garden, where a series of wooden Doric columns, wound about with ivy and wisteria, stand like statues against the sides and back of the boundary walls. Occasional benches and seats are inter-

spersed between the columns, behind which more vines climb lattice attatched to the walls. Gravel paths divide the columned alcoves from a central rectangular bed of ivy underplanted with miniature daffodils, which spreads beneath the great sycamore at the back of the garden.

Although the garden has a strong formal structure, the solitary columns, half obscured by vines, suggest an atmosphere of abandonment, a feeling that you have entered a secret, romantic ruin of a garden. "We were so lucky to find those old columns at a wrecking company. New ones would not have worked—what I didn't want were perfect proportions." This sense of imperfection, of "order humanized," pleases Madison. He feels this garden typifies his best work—the creative transformation of a very structured space: "I tweak it so it's not so stiff and cold."

For two avid Francophiles in Manhattan, Dorothy Hamilton and her husband, Madison designed a garden on several levels behind a brownstone, creating a very French sense of order that he then softened with plantings. "I love French gardens, but they have a severe quality that I sometimes find too hard." The clients wanted a bocce court on the ground level of their garden

like the ones they had seen in France, and they wanted the atmosphere of a French courtyard. Madison raised the level of the backyard, originally "a brick pit," so that it became an extension of the dining room. He covered the ground with fine gravel and planted four large sycamores in a rectangle to define the garden. The house was completely gutted when the Hamiltons began their renovation and discovered that the building's underpinnings were rotten. One lucky result was that, because there were no interior walls, Madison was able to bring in unusually big trees. "We had a clear shot from the street through a forty-inch-wide window [the width of the window determined the size of the root balls], and we rolled the trees right in through the house."

The trees were planted directly in the gravel, as you would see them in a French park. The effect is clean-looking, and quite striking, even in winter. Madison stuccoed the perimeter walls that surround the garden and added lattice on top for more height and privacy. Extremely narrow perimeter beds at the foot of the walls provide room for vines—climbing hydrangea (a favorite of Madison's, but difficult to use, he says, because its slow initial growth frustrates impatient

and adding to its feeling of serene formality. Madison envisions that, in a few years' time, the garden will have a "feeling of entanglement, an overgrown quality" as the formal lines become half-obscured by the vines. "I guess one of the effects that I love most is that of a secret garden, somewhat abandoned and overgrown. In a proper French garden you wouldn't expect to find that sort of atmosphere."

Nevertheless, "this is an extremely minimal, low-maintenance garden for very busy people," Madison says. "It's a simple solution for people who want their garden to look good all year 'round." In the city, he explained, spaces are very confined and clients want their gardens to look their best in the fall, winter, and spring. There is a greater emphasis on evergreens, on pots and containers, and more need for formality in design. And invariably, Madison added, annuals are relied on for seasonal color.

On the rooftop of the Hamiltons' house, Madison designed a "Villandry sort of thing," a pattern of planters exclusively for vegetables and herbs. Mrs. Hamilton, who is the founder of the French Culinary Institute, wanted a place where she could grow a few vegetables and flavorings for her own kitchen. Madison planted crab apple trees in boxes to surround and shade a dining table and chairs, and two boxes of wisteria to train along the latticed fence that encloses the area. The rest of the garden was plotted out with seasonal plantings of lettuce, corn, tomatoes, and other vegetables. Now Mrs. Hamilton has taken over the annual planting of the boxes. Because this is strictly a summer garden and the owners don't go up to the roof in winter, the fact that it is composed mostly of tender annuals doesn't matter. The year-round focus from the house is on the main formal garden. "From the dining room, you look under the sycamores to the fountain. One level up, in the living room, you feel you are in the trees." How a garden looks from indoors is an essential concern of Madison's.

clients), ivy, and sweet autumn clematis. Two benches face each other across the central gravel court, and a French cafe table and chairs invite lingering in the center of the garden. The far wall, facing the house, was built up with stucco to ten feet and laced with more vines. Here, a stone fountain, mounted on the wall, ends the main garden axis, providing that essential plashing of water. Clipped balls of Japanese holly in large Portland stone pots stand around the edges of the courtyard, breaking the linear severity of the design

LEFT: *Corn flourishes in a wooden planter on this East Side Manhattan rooftop.*
BELOW: *Young crab apples, underplanted with* fraises du bois, *shade a table for alfresco meals among the vegetables and herbs. Espaliered pear trees are trained up a lattice fence for privacy.*

One of his first projects in New York was a collaborative effort with the artist Jennifer Bartlett, designing her infinitely more complex garden on several levels of rooftop in Greenwich Village. The layout for the garden has basically remained unchanged from Madison's original conception, but the actual planting was delayed and revised several times. The transformation of what was an old railroad warehouse into Bartlett's studio and living quarters (including a lap pool on the top floor) were unexpectedly complicated and prolonged. The indoor rooms were designed with views of the garden in mind, for Bartlett wanted "gardenscapes that would be totally integrated with the interior living spaces."

The layout of the planting beds was constrained by the load limits of the building roof top, and required the help and approval of several structural engineers. In the end, forty-two tons of soil were used, as well as two tons of bricks and stone dust and hundreds of plants (trees, shrubs, perennials and annuals).

Galvanized steel planters ("easy-care, but they bake in summer") were built for all the plantings, some almost three feet deep, others as shallow as nine inches. They form a "labyrinth of garden rooms, each half-hidden from the next to increase the fun of discovery." Formal parterres of boxwood and specimen conifers surround a seating area off the living room level, enclosed by walls of perforated cinder block covered with cream-colored stucco and laced with wisteria and clematis. The walls provide privacy while the pattern of small square openings gives them an appearance of airiness. At the end of the main axis, a modernistic wall-mounted

fountain spills water into a trough filled with koi, masking with its splashing sound the persistent hum of neighboring air conditioners. An iron spiral staircase and catwalk wound round with flowering vines lead to the top floor level—the most private area—where crab apples and an arbor of blush pink roses shade a terrace off the pool and, in the blazing sun on either side, shrub roses spill lushly out of deep containers. It is astonishing to stand in the space, awash in the luxuriousness of roses and herbs, and realize that you are in the middle of a city where outlines of tall buildings surround you.

A diamond-patterned garden of inkberry, which, in its maturity, is now an evergreen maze, leads out from one end of the glass-doored pool room. At the other end, ornamental grasses wave in a long narrow bed. The grasses replaced a garden of lavender that failed, and the inkberry was preceded by heathers that refused to thrive. The harshness of the weather on top of

PRECEDING PAGES *and* FAR LEFT: *A bird's-eye view of artist Jennifer Bartlett's rooftop garden. Creating the garden was a collaborative effort between the artist and Madison.* LEFT: *A spiral staircase and catwalk, cloaked with wisteria and 'New Dawn' roses, leads to the top and most private level of the garden.* ABOVE: *A long bed of grasses beside pillars of yew extends out to beds of shrub roses in the sunniest area of the garden.* ABOVE RIGHT *and* RIGHT: *Squares of inkberry,* Ilex glabra, *creating a maze, have replaced a garden of heathers that failed to survive the rigors of the rooftop.*

a city roof makes gardening there a gamble. As in gardens everywhere, its failures teach you to settle for those plants that flourish in your particular environment.

Madison says the design of the garden would have been much more formal without Bartlett's input. "Her way is more contemporary—she's not getting out her T square," he said with a grin. "I learned a lot working with her." As Madison wrote in his book, *Artists' Gardens,* "When an artist looks at a garden, the first thing to go is convention—suddenly there are no rules, and this above all is one of the most liberating of experiences for a trained garden designer."

One of the most frustrating experiences for an urban designer planning a terrace or roof garden is dealing with the demands of a building's superintendent. A terrace overlooking the East River that Madison worked on recently is a prime example of what he calls "the nightmare of working in New York City." The client wanted a garden on the terrace that wrapped around her apartment, but the building manager refused to allow any permanent structures because of the threat of lawsuits if there were to be any water damage. Madison worked with structural engineers for two years before he was allowed to proceed with twelve shallow planter boxes. "They weren't deep enough for anything but annuals, so I decided to make them wacky-looking." Their striking appearance insures visual interest even in wintertime. The white-painted wooden boxes are fanciful, flared like vases with fat balled feet, and in the summer are filled with lush mixtures of tender plants in blue, white, and green. "The planter boxes are as important as what's in them. They are almost like theater sets." Looking very much on the bright side, Madison adds, "Projects like this can be fun"—especially when viewed in retrospect!

To some extent, all Madison's city gardens are like theater sets. His strong, formal lines of paths and walls, softened by rows of trees and vine-laden lattices, his columns and splashing fountains, are the serene backdrops for the pots of seasonal flowers, the tapestries of bulbs that come up through the ground covers, and, of course, the owners themselves, who, with their guests, enliven his gardens. That those stage sets are lived in, that his gardens are used, is important to Madison. It reminds him of the Mogul gardens he loves, where people feel welcome to linger, to rest and to eat, enjoying the garden as a refuge from the heat and bustle just outside its walls.

LEFT: *Madison designed flaring wooden pots with balled feet, painted creamy white, to look good—even when empty in winter—on this East River terrace.* **ABOVE** *and* **RIGHT:** *"There is a greater emphasis on pots of evergreens and annuals in the city," Madison says, "and more reliance on formality, because we are dealing with such confined spaces."*

Patrick Chassé

Patrick Chassé

W HEN PATRICK CHASSÉ TACKLES a new garden project, he begins by thinking about rock. Whether discovered on site, exposed, or imported from elsewhere, rock, enlivened with water and softened with native plantings, is the springboard of his garden designs and often its most essential feature.

Patrick's affinity for rock and his genius for its use comes partly from a lifelong appreciation of Oriental garden aesthetics. In the Eastern tradition of copying nature's forms and textures, stone and water are all-important. Rock is stripped of embellishment in the harsh, primal Chinese expression of landscape; in the more tranquil Japanese interpretation, it is softened with an overlay of planting.

The fiercely ragged coast of northeastern Maine, Patrick's native landscape, also feeds his passion for stone. The peculiar beauty of this part of the world lies in the contrast between the crude and dramatic rock-bound shoreline, lapped by a cold sapphire sea, and the soft, luxuriant vegetation flourishing against it. Richly colored firs and spruce grow thickly up to the granite-littered shore; beneath them, carpets of low-growing blueberry bushes (called blueberry sod by nurserymen), bunchberry, sweet fern, and moss paint the ground in tones of emerald green. What more natural place to suggest an Oriental approach to gardening?

In fact, Patrick's home ground on Mount Desert Island has been a hotbed of Japanese and Chinese garden influences for many decades. John D. Rockefeller, Jr., started it all when he brought his family to the island at the begining of the century. He asked the great American garden designer Beatrix Farrand, who was also a resident, to collaborate with his wife, Abby, in creating a garden that would combine Asian and Western elements.

Patrick, much influenced by Farrand, and involved today in the restoration of the Rockefeller garden, describes it as "a meeting of East and West...applying an English garden tradition within an Oriental framework,

PRECEDING PAGES: *At Salt Ponds, an idyllic retreat on an island off the coast of northern Maine, Patrick Chassé captured the essence of a Japanese garden with rock, water, and carpets of native mosses and blueberries. From the house, a path leads to an arched bridge across a swale, and continues on to a boulder-strewn beach and the ocean. "East meets West, on the East Coast," is how Patrick wryly describes his garden designs.* LEFT: *Wooly thyme flows along a stone path through Chinese junipers and mugo pines to a hidden garden in Winter Harbor, Maine.*

A view of Thuya Garden on Mount Desert Island through borders of softly colored perennials and annuals to a rustic pavilion. Patrick restored the plantings in the tradition of Beatrix Farrand (and her mentor, Gertrude Jekyll), with a succession of colors from warm to cool. With the warm colors in the foreground of this view progressing to cool colors, the length of the allée is exaggerated, and the pavilion is made to seem more remote. Looking at the garden from the pavilion, the warm colors in the distance seem to come forward, compressing the length of the double border.

built in a strong natural setting." It is a garden sensitive to its magnificent surroundings, and at the same time succeeds in expressing two seemingly opposite aesthetics. Fresh from travels in China and Japan, the Rockefellers created a woodland sculpture garden where life-size Chinese-style stone figures stand in native mosses on either side of a walk they called the Spirit Path. From here, a cross path leads to a large, sunlit, geometric garden of flowers.

For Mrs. Rockefeller wanted not only an Oriental-style garden, she wanted beds of flowers. It was up to Beatrix Farrand to devise a way of visually segregating these two disparate parts of the garden. This she did with low walls and soft plantings of rugosa roses. A high Chinese tile-capped wall was later built to enclose the whole garden, with gated openings designed in intricate detail by Farrand. These serve as appealing entrances from the surrounding woodland, framing vistas, like poetic paintings, of the garden. Once within the enveloping wall, you realize that the garden diffuses subtly from its strict geometric center to the winding Oriental paths and finally to the lush natural landscape beyond.

Farrand's influence also is evident at nearby Thuya Garden, set high above Northeast Harbor, where Patrick has recently refurbished the plantings. It is a garden that has inspired Patrick since he first discovered it as a high-school student in the 1960s. "I was hiking on one of the woodland paths and came to a wooden gate, beautifully crafted of see-through squares. Inside was a garden, but no sign of people. I opened the gate and walked in, and my jaw dropped. It was a wonderful place, a quiet, highly ordered flower garden that blended seamlessly into the natural landscape. I wasn't conscious of why it worked, but I was deeply moved. Thinking it was a private garden, I took one panoramic look, then crept away."

Patrick soon learned that he had not been trespassing—that indeed this magical place was open to the public, thanks to the legacy of its first owner, the landscape architect Joseph Henry Curtis. The central garden at Thuya was created in the 1950s by Charles Savage, a local artist, woodcarver, and garden designer who was a friend and disciple of Beatrix Farrand. Many of the plants at Thuya came from Farrand's own nearby garden, Reef Point, which was being dismantled at that time. Although Savage had studied Oriental landscape theory and was influenced by it in his design, he saw Thuya primarily as an English or Western garden set in the native landscape he knew and loved so well. The garden today is approached by car up a steep, curving driveway through woodland strewn with ledges so magnificent Patrick brings his clients to see them as a separate attraction from the garden. He hopes this will educate them in the beauties of the area's indigenous rock. A small parking area just outside the garden allows visitors to enter through large wooden gates designed by Savage and hand-carved with local plant and animal motifs.

Curtis landscaped another route to his lodge to be traversed on foot rather than by carriage or car, which adds immeasurably to one's sense of suprise and delight upon discovery of this garden. From the dock down by the shore a path wends its way up Asticou Hill through a series of stone terraces and steps. Rustic shelters with seats allow you to rest along the way and offer glimpses of the harbor below. At the end of this enticing climb you enter Savage's dreamlike garden of sunlight and repose. A hip-roofed garden structure shading wicker chairs (suggestive of a Japanese tea house) looks out over the long main axis, down granite steps, and through a pair of softly colored flower borders to a rock-bound, gourd-shaped pond set just slightly off-center. Groves of native wildflowers and shrubs surround this formal center. Like the Rockefeller garden, Thuya is enclosed, but with a northern white cedar fence (Thuya was named after the northern white cedar trees, *Thuja occidentalis,* that grow there). This fence, with the massed native perimeter plantings that surround it, makes a sympathetic transition to the embracing woodland. Charles Savage had learned from Beatrix Farrand how to blend the garden styles of East and West, and how to marry the formal with the informal. Their influence is evident in all of Patrick Chassé's gardens.

Even in the lushness of the plantings at Thuya and the Rockefeller gardens, you are aware of strong rock underpinnings—the ledges, boulders, paths, and steps that interrupt the plantings and speak of Maine and its shoreline. Water is the other invariable feature, whether in naturalistic rivulets, or formal pools, or glimpses of the ocean. Always, the woodland is ever-present, with its rich evergreens and verdant ground covers. These three elements—rock, water, and woodland—are Patrick's preferred palette, the soul of his gardens.

The moss garden Patrick created at Salt Ponds on Long Island, ten miles out into the ocean from Northeast Harbor, is a prime illustration of his work. Called in to help in the siting and construction of a Japanese-style residence and to create a sympathetic surrounding landscape, Patrick naturally started with stone. He persuaded the builders of this elegant lodge to dispense with wooden latticework they intended to erect to screen the foundation, a change which allowed the house to seemingly float on its narrow platform like a hovercraft. A drip line around the structure was laid with handsome stone and gravel, serving also as a path, and large rectangular stepping stones were artfully placed in tiers to reach the house from the surrounding land. The house was sited so that the windows on all four sides would offer panoramic views of ocean, salt ponds, woodland, and garden. Thinking about "what could be developed out of whole cloth," the same types of stones Patrick used outside the house for steps and paths were used inside to fashion the fireplace. The canoe birches he clustered in groves around the house also echo the charcoal-flecked, creamy white birch panels that line the living-room walls.

Patrick came across this open-squared gate when hiking in the woods on Mount Desert Island as a boy. He was astonished to find within the cedar fencing a quiet, highly ordered flower garden that appeared to blend seamlessly into the surrounding landscape. This was his introduction to the magic of Thuya, the garden created in the 1950s by Charles Savage, friend and disciple of Beatrix Farrand.
FOLLOWING PAGES: *The Japanese-style lodge at Salt Ponds seems to float over the stone and moss that covers the ground.*

Patrick was not interested in making an authentic Japanese garden for his clients' retreat, but rather in capturing the essence of such a garden. "I don't attempt to copy Chinese or Japanese gardens. I use their precepts as a basis for my design, then build upon those ideas with the house, the site, and the native landscape in mind. East meets West…on the East Coast," he says with a smile.

At Salt Ponds, he started the garden by studying the rock underpinnings. He stripped away earth "down to the armature" to expose the existing ledge rock, then brought more boulders over from the mainland to extend the revealed spine and mold his landscape. Water now trickles down these rocks into natural-looking pools, recirculated by a hidden pump and pipes. Patrick then clothed the rolling contours of the surrounding land with vast carpets of moss and blueberry sod. He

lined a drainage gully so naturalistically with stone it looks like a stream bed gone dry. A five-foot-wide crushed granite path wends serenely through a red and white spruce forest to the house, finally swirling around a mammoth rock like a Japanese sand garden. "My intention was for the garden to read both ways—Oriental and natural. The house triggers an Oriental response, and I wanted the serenity of a Japanese garden, its scale and massing. But if the house ever burned down you would think the landscape around it was natural."

Patrick is meticulous about details. An outdoor seating terrace is sunk below ground level so that it doesn't disturb the views of ocean and mossy woodland. A gently arching silver-hued bridge connects a path over a natural swale to one side of the house. In the Farrand style, Patrick made a mock-up of the bridge first in plywood to be sure the scale was right, and even painted it gray so it would look like the final faded wooden version.

The plant list for Salt Ponds was short, consisting almost entirely of natives of the island, such as sheep laurel, juniper, and low-bush blueberry. But an unexpected problem with deer swimming ashore has shortened the list even more. The spruce and birch endure, and, happily, the deer don't eat the velvet moss, which is "sublime at its best" in early summer.

In Japan, Patrick says, horsetail and siver cushion mosses are used extensively in garden design. In the West, "they're left in the dust." One problem is that you have to match the microhabitat to the specific moss that suits it, and in order to identify and know your mosses, you have to be a bit of a botanist. This is no problem for Patrick, because his graduate-school training was in botany.

While a biology student at the University of Maine, Patrick worked for two summers on cancer research at the Jackson Laboratory on Mount Desert Island and there had the good fortune to meet Janet Tenbroeck. With two colleagues, she had founded Wild Gardens of Arcadia to preserve and display native ferns, and asked Patrick to help identify hybrid ferns for her organization. This led Patrick to a more scholarly appreciation of native flora and to his first involvement in creating designs for local gardens. It was a turning point in his life, for Patrick realized he wanted to work out in the field, not in a laboratory, in a way that married science and art. He had gardened since he was a boy, and had always loved to draw and paint. He decided to go back to school at Harvard to get a masters degree in landscape design, and then to settle permanently on Mount Desert Island.

Mrs. Tenbroeck had also kindled Patrick's interest in the Orient with stories of Peking, where she had lived for several years with her husband, and Patrick started to make periodic trips to China and Japan to study gardens there. The Chinese gardens shocked him at first—the grotesque, baroque rockeries were so different from anything we are accustomed to. He felt more comfortable

LEFT: *Rather than standing his client's eight Korean tomb figures in a ceremonial line, Patrick placed them among granite boulders "so they look like they're a part of the natural rock that came alive. This is not a Japanese concept at all,"* he is quick to add. ABOVE: *You approach the lodge at Salt Ponds through a woodland of spruce, birch, moss, and rock, along a crushed granite path that finally swirls around a boulder—as in a Japanese sand garden.* RIGHT: *From a gravel and stone path that follows the drip line, more stones are arranged as steps to reach the veranda surrounding the house.*

with the Japanese aesthetic, in which the bones of Chinese ideas were softened with plantings. But he feels he learned from the Chinese how to distill the basic forms of nature, to appreciate simplification. "In Japan," Patrick says, "the essence of garden art is rooted in the deep understanding of natural scenery," and this is certainly a precept of Patrick's garden designs. But Patrick's style is looser and freer. He enjoys the natural forms of plants rather than the clipped, controlled tailoring of a Japanese garden.

The Asticou Azalea Garden, in Northeast Harbor, which Patrick helped restore and extend, although Japanese in feeling, is infinitely more relaxed. ("The Japanese would think it ragged.") Like Thuya, Asticou was originally designed in the 1950s by Charles Savage to house a collection of azaleas and native plants from Farrand's dismantled garden at Reef Point. In the early 1980s, Patrick was called in by the Island Foundation, which now owns Asticou, to restore the deteriorated plantings, create a new public entrance, and devise a

path system through what is essentially a stroll garden. Using crushed pink granite, Patrick designed the paths "to flow like calligraphy," looping past the lily pond and moss garden, across bridges made of ledgerock to the sand garden and Great Pond. He found marvelous pieces of granite to use as stepping stones, then clothed the sides of his paths with flowing sheets of bunchberry, wild ginger, wintergreen, and different mosses and ferns. Shadbushes and enkianthus, sheep laurel and blueberry were planted by a new gated entrance. As at the moss garden, one notes the attention to detail that makes a Chassé garden special.

In Winter Harbor, Maine, Patrick was asked to design a small garden for an Oriental-style house ("more Thai than Japanese") sited by a bay. The clients wanted a Japanese garden and an English herbaceous border not unlike the combination requested by the Rockefellers fifty years earlier, but on a much more modest scale. Using as inspiration a Chinese export

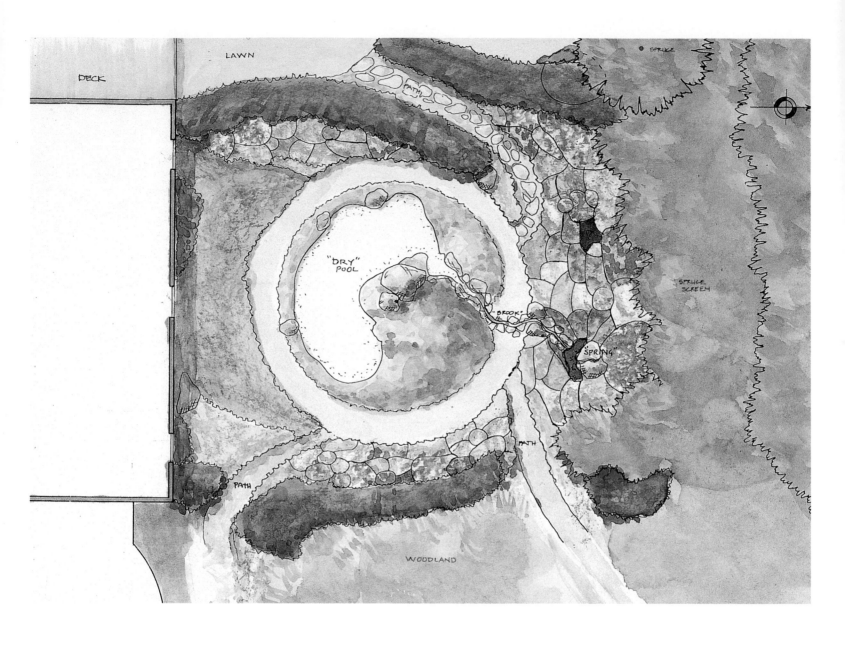

Image labels: DECK, LAWN, SPRUCE, PATH, "DRY" POOL, BROOK, SPRING, SPRUCE SCREEN, PATH, PATH, WOODLAND

porcelain bowl he remembered seeing at the Museum of Fine Arts in Boston, which had a scene in the bottom and a floral pattern on the rim, Patrick designed a circular landscape of rock, water, and pea gravel as the center of the garden. Around this he devised a pea gravel path and then a border of flowers, like the decorative edging on the bowl.

Patrick surrounded the Bowl Garden with a hedge of mugo pines, so that the garden is invisible until entered, and he filled in the natural backdrop of spruce trees with similar smaller specimens. From the water, the house appears to be simply embraced by native ever-

ABOVE *and* **TOP RIGHT**: *Patrick designed this small circular garden for an Oriental-style house in Winter Harbor, Maine, where the owners wanted both a Japanese garden and flower borders. Basing the garden on a Chinese porcelain bowl depicting a landscape in* *the center and a floral pattern on the rim, Patrick created a small circle of rock, water, and pea gravel planted with thyme and creeping junipers, and surrounded it with a path and borders of flowers.* **BOTTOM RIGHT**: *The Bowl Garden is hidden from the ocean front by mugo pines.*

greens. But as you walk through a gap in that voluptuous green wall just outside the house, you enter a fantasy garden of sculptured stone and sand, rampant now with woolly thyme and creeping junipers and ribboned by tall-growing delphiniums, thalictrums, and cow parsley.

One of the challenges for all garden designers lies in suiting the garden to the house and, at the same time, meeting the requirements and demands of the clients. A recent challenge that Patrick has found exciting has been creating an appropriate garden around a Greek

temple built as a weekend home in a woodland an hour north of New York City.

The house, designed by the architects Patrick Naggar and Therese Carpenter, is a stunning rendition of a Doric temple, built of weathered cedar rather than marble. In the same vein, Patrick has used Grecian structures as the bones of his garden, but simplified them by using rustic materials more sympathetic to the site. For the entrance to the house, Patrick leveled and sculpted a circular courtyard inspired by the Greek

amphitheater at Epidaurus. Granite stones radiate out from a Renaissance well in the center of the circle. Raised beds all around the perimeter, like seating platforms, are contained by granite curbs and backed by a stepped planting of rhododendrons set against a tall clipped hemlock hedge. A collection of busts on columns peer out from the bushes, "like an audience of immortals watching the mortals arrive." Patrick imported huge slabs of ledge rock from Pennsylvania to make a series of steps leading up from the parking area through an opening in the hemlock hedge. Here the temple is suddenly revealed as you step down into the courtyard, on an axis with the front door.

On the south side of the house, an elegant stone terrace of bluestone squares, set on the diagonal and broken by two ancient crab apples, leads to a long lap pool lined in black. The pool is designed with a spillway all around so that the water can flow over its edges, giving the illusion of a mirror. Along one length of the pool, a pergola was fashioned of rustic white cedar columns and beams that Patrick had brought down from Maine.

ABOVE LEFT: *With humor and inventiveness, Patrick created a grotto beneath a formal swimming pool he designed for clients who had just built an elegant Doric temple as their weekend home outside of New York City. You approach the grotto on stepping stones* *across a pond Patrick dredged and lined with huge boulders and ferns. Recirculating water spills over the rocks into the pond.* RIGHT: *The interior walls of the grotto are fiberglass cast from real ledge rock by a former model maker at the Museum of Natural History in New York.*

Beneath the pool, Patrick made a secret grotto, a "nymphaeum," with a round window offering a glimpse into the pool. Another window in the ceiling of the grotto looks up through the glass bottom of a small circular fountain pool placed at the end of the long pool axis. (All that is lacking, Patrick wryly suggested to his client, are some local nymphs.)

The interior walls of the grotto are covered with fiberglass ledge rock cast from real ledge rock by a former model maker at the American Museum of Natural History in New York City. Outside, true boulders have been brought in to clothe the entrance and edge a small natural-looking pond, which was excavated and built up with shale. The only way to get into the "nymphaeum" is along stepping stones placed across this pond. The woodland beyond the pond and surrounding the house has massed plantings of native flora, along with vast sweeps of daffodils, blurring the edges between cultivated and wild.

Patrick has been involved in the development of another, albeit simpler, garden outside of New York City that incorporates pools, ponds, and woodland. The unpretentious one-story house sits on ledge rock high up among oak trees and luxuriant rhododendrons

ABOVE: A pergola, fashioned of white cedar timber brought down from Maine, shades one side of the new lap pool, which Patrick designed with a spillway on all four sides. The water, level with the surrounding paving, flows over the edges of the spillway, creating a mirror-like effect. RIGHT: In another New York country garden, Patrick arranged boulders around a man-made pond to seem as if they had tumbled down the hill.

overlooking a serene willow-framed pond. A meandering rock-bound path and steps lead down from the house to a swimming pool on one side and a sweep of lawn and garden on the other. I was startled to learn that Patrick had trucked stone in for that path; it had seemed perfectly natural. "I wanted it to look like a glacier had just tumbled stone down the hill."

Patrick replaced the diving board of the swimming pool with a diving rock—merely a large flat rock jutting into the water. "A Zen diving board," he calls it. The paving around the pool is now interrupted by boulders, as

though they were there first and the pool was built around them. Allowing rock to "tumble out and back across the pool" gives the impression that "nature still dominates."

Stones were also put along the banks of the man-made pond, as though it were "pulling boulders down from the hill." Massed perennials (astilbes, cranesbills, hostas) divide the curve of lawn from the woodland; Patrick then added an understory of native shrubs to blend the edges of the garden seamlessly into the landscape.

Patrick likes to compare this garden to another he is helping to restore on the North Shore above Boston.

Originally designed by Frederick Law Olmsted, Jr., it is a formal geometric garden of pools and plantings, stone walls and steps, terraced down a slope from the Edwardian house to ocean on one side and woods on the other. Both this and the New York garden have a setting of rocks and pools, an important view of water, and an enveloping woodland. But here in the Olmsted garden, the bones are grand and formal. Patrick was called in to overlay the old design with new plantings, bringing a modern sensibility to an Edwardian garden originally built for summer use only.

The new full-time owners approached Patrick after seeing his sensitive refurbishment of the flower garden at Thuya, in Maine. He had recently updated and refined the borders there, combining Farrand's feeling for color (warm yellows fading into creams and pinks, lengthening to lavender blues and silver) with his own flair for texture and pattern.

Using the same concept, Patrick introduced a new, more fluid planting of shrubs, perennials, grasses, and annuals to the Olmsted garden in a Farrand-like succession of soft colors. The garden now appears refreshed and full of interest year-round. "Everybody thinks architecture in a garden is anathema today," Patrick complains. "On the contrary, geometry gives pure pleasure." Curvy beds near a formal house can, ironically, seem stiff and contrived. As the revived Olmsted garden recedes from the house, however, Patrick has added his signature sweep of naturalistic plantings, bleeding the garden into the woodland.

ABOVE: *In a garden on the North Shore of Boston, originally designed for summer use by Frederick Law Olmstead, Jr., Patrick planted borders of ornamental grasses and perennials (in segregated colors from blue to pink to yellow) to be visually pleasing from the house all year.* LEFT: *The soft lavender flowers of creeping thyme echo and enhance the vibrant purple hues of the Japanese iris in the formal water garden.*

Patrick is always stressing the importance of edges in garden design—what he calls the transition between art and nature. "There is always a place for a flower garden, no matter how contrived. The key is that all these human expressions—house, garden—are inlays within a larger natural context. It is the edges that determine the harmony and how it works."

Whether it is bunchberry feathered out into a woodland floor of pine needles, laurel and viburnum bled into an understory of oaks, or rock tumbling down a hillside, these are Patrick's ways of blending his garden art into the natural landscape.

Alain David Idoux

Alain David Idoux

THE LUBERON REGION OF PROVENCE, east of Avignon, where designer Alain Idoux lives, presents a breathtakingly picturesque composition of wild and cultivated land. Oaks, pines, and boxwood clothe great swaths of the steep, craggy mountainsides, giving way to rock-studded moorland of yellow-flowering gorse and aromatic herbs. This the French call the *garrigue*, a place where the soil is so thin and dry only low vegetation survives. Turn a bend in the road, however, and the wild limestone landscape suddenly meets vasts grids of

lavender—row upon row of mounded lavender plants, slate blue in July, steel gray in the spring—swooping down into the valleys. The lavender fields in turn give way to vineyards, also in satisfying geometric profiles, and, along the fertile valleys, to orchards of cherry trees and almonds. Walled medieval villages, perched like rock outcroppings on the mountain heights, fall away to terraced groves of olive trees among tumbling rock, broom, and boxwood. It is this juxtaposition of rugged untamed land and cultivated patterns of farming that continually startles and delights the eye.

The Vaucluse, as this department of Provence is called, is ancient farming land. Vineyards, olives, sheep, and herbs have supported the economy of the region for centuries. Only now, in the twentieth century, is this farmland, along with the native flora, threatened by rampant tourism and urbanization.

When Alain describes gardening in Provence, he speaks of "taming the *garrigue*." But in fact, he is passionate about the wildness of his countryside, and is only interested in partially taming it. The simplicity of the *garrigue,* with its predominance of rock and rugged

PRECEDING PAGES: *To take advantage of a view at La Chabaude, his* bastide *in the Luberon region of Provence, Alain Idoux fashioned a rugged bench and terrace out of stone, then planted cypresses for punctuation and a hackberry tree for eventual shade.*
RIGHT: *Alain's background as a sculptor is evident from the way he sites artifacts, stones, or fragments of Roman ruins at the ends of axes, marking perspectives in his gardens. Here, he found the stone edge of an old well and set it vertically on a base to frame a view and catch your eye beyond a narrow walk through billowing clumps of herbs at La Chabaude.*

unkempt beauty, appeals to Alain's aesthetic. Born in Marseilles, Alain grew up in a landscape of limestone cliffs. With his family, he spent many childhood years in Provence and vividly remembers planting, with his father, one hundred almond trees.

Later, in his twenties, he fell in love with the starkness of a truly arid landscape, that of the desert in Israel, where he studied and taught sculpture for eight years. Alain returned to France to exhibit a sculpture at the Pompidou Center in Paris and ended up staying. He thinks of that sculpture as a turning toward the land and his future involvement in it. "It was an environmental piece, columns of clay that took up the whole room. There was a system of dripping water on some of the columns and the columns were unfired. By the end of the exhibit, some of the columns were nothing but mud on the ground. So it was a work about time and the different states of clay, whether mud or dry."

Alain went on to teach sculpture at the Beaux Arts in Caen, Normandy. "Each year, I had a student project in the countryside. I would teach the students how to develop a concept that related to nature. Any material could be land art, made of objects found on the earth." During his final year of teaching he led a seminar that he called "The Relationship between Artist and Nature." Each student had to work on two sites. "One site was very chaotic, along the ocean; the second site was a garden, a very beautiful eighteenth-century garden called Canon Mezidon. For me it was a revelation. I was so excited to work in a garden. I decided to stop teaching, give up my job—I had tenure—return to Provence, and try to design gardens."

Alain learned from Nicole de Vesian the basics of gardening in the Provençal landscape, and was deeply influenced by the simplicity and purity of her stunning architectural garden style using sculpted herbs and stones. But Alain's gardens are not so controlled. "I love the contrast between the controlled and the wild," he says—playing flowers, for example, against those clipped herbs and stones.

Alain studied the land and the trees by himself, learning from books. At first, still sculpting for a living, he started designing small gardens. Gradually, through word-of-mouth and articles in magazines, Alain's work as a designer got to be known, and eventually he was designing gardens full time. "Some of my clients were very open-minded. I could tell them about land art and little by little introduce sculpture to the land." He calls it "putting signs in the landscape."

That Alain is a sculptor has everything to do with his method of designing a garden. An ideal situation, he says, is to work on a garden slowly for several years (one needs a patient client), first cleaning the site, clearing out weedy growth, exposing the structure of good trees, getting a sense of the land. Next, Alain likes to set some stones (they might be Roman ruins or just rocks lying about) as sculptures, moving them around a few times until he marks the perspectives he wants in the garden. "You punctuate the space with mineral elements that attract the eye," he explains. Then he thinks about the plantings. To help develop a concept for the garden, he takes a series of photographs of the different areas to be designed, taping them together to make panoramas of each area. These he tacks up on boards in his studio so that even when he is working on another project he will see them. Then, as ideas take shape in his head, he sketches with pastels on tracing paper laid over the panoramas, drawing in the trees and sculpture and flowers that he visualizes in the space. When he is satisfied with his concept, he shows the colored drawings to his clients for approval.

Alain's own garden at La Chabaude, an eighteenth-century *bastide* above the town of Apt, has grown in a more impromptu fashion, and, indeed, he thinks of it as his laboratory. The garden was in ruins when he moved there in 1990—vines and weeds obliterating the walls, festooning the trees, and choking the ground. But there were olive trees dotting the fields, and a beautiful view across the hills, and a sense that

When developing an idea for a garden, Alain takes a series of photographs of the site, which he tapes together to create a panorama. Then he lays tracing paper over the photographs and, with pastels, sketches his ideas for the garden. Here, plans for a jardin de senteurs, a herb and flower garden, at a house in the Alpilles.

the old manor house had once had a certain elegance and charm.

Alain began by clearing around the house, exposing its buff-colored walls and gently arched windows. A handsome piered gateway and high courtyard wall were discovered underneath the vines on the more formal south front of the *bastide*. Ancient sycamores just outside the gate were cleaned of debris, and a path now wends its way downhill beneath their dramatically spreading limbs.

Alain cleaned up the walled courtyard entrance to the house, laid down gravel, and set long natural stones

as steps to the high arched doorway. To one side he created a small bench out of three large stones and planted silver-leaved teucrium on each side, which he then clipped into balls. Turning down the gift of a stereo from a friend, he asked for a cypress tree instead, and planted it against the house to one side of the stone bench, where it serves as a striking vertical accent. Two shaped bay laurels now stand on either side of the door, and mounds of myrtle flourish by the steps. In essence, he sculpted this first garden area with plants and stones.

Looking out from the front door across the gravel yard, you can catch a glimpse of a sculpture at the end of an axis that leads through the wooden gate in the courtyard wall and down a graveled path. The sculpture is in the shape of a finial, made from an old stone Alain found and propped up on a stone block between two young oak trees, with a background of blue hills. It is one of the many perspectives Alain has created in his garden, always in a slightly offhand way, surprising you as you turn a corner, pleasing your eye.

Alain designed a severely simple lap pool at La Chabaude, then softened it with lush plantings of rosemary, lavender, pittosporum, box honeysuckle, and a feathery tamarisk tree. Cypresses and a metal sculpture of Alain's at the end of the pool axis add the desired vertical notes.

One of his own metal sculptures, U-shaped and red with rust, stands at the end of the long lap pool he designed, and enfolds the view beyond. The pool is almost severe in its clean-lined simplicity except for two feathery tamarisk trees that cut its strict geometric lines, offering shade for alfresco meals. On one side of the pool, a retaining wall holds a succession of clipped and spilling herbs and shrubs—rosemary, santolina, sweet bay, pittosporum, box honeysuckle, laurustinus—punctuated by a series of cypress, and this planting serves as a luxuriant screen from the house entrance. On the other side of the pool, lavender billows into the water.

Looser, more colorful flowers mingle with clipped herbs in garden beds below the pool. Poppies and sage, perovskia, gaura, yarrow, senecio, round bushes of hypericum, all thrive with little care in the hot, dry Provence climate. Alain fashioned a massive, high-backed bench out of local stone among these flowers, offering a stunning view of the mountains that makes you want to linger. A small *micocoulier,* or hackberry, Alain's favorite tree, was planted near the bench for shade, and a few cypresses were added to punctuate the view. One Fourth of July evening, when I was visiting, Alain placed torches in the garden beds so that we could eat dinner on the bench under a vast sky of stars, celebrating America's independence with a bottle of champagne. He delights in eating in unexpected places in his garden, often carrying a small table and café chairs to a new spot to take advantage of a certain perspective or atmosphere. Gardens, as far as Alain is concerned, are to be used.

The most recent experiment in land art at La Chabaude is a large stone circle in the sloping field above the house. Alain explains its concept: "The field was full of stones left over from rebuilding the house, and it was a problem because the field was difficult to mow. I had to get rid of the stones. My bedroom window faces the field, and I thought if I used the stones to make a sign that I could see from my bed it would make me feel good." Because the field slants toward the house, any structure there would be fully visible. Alain rejected the idea of a rectangle ("All is curved here," he notes), deciding instead on a circle, a "more neutral sign." Slowly, he moved the broken limestones scattered in the field until they formed a large ghostly ring. At a point in the circle near the house, a small oak tree stood, "quite by magic. I don't know how it survived—we burned the field originally. I decided to venerate this little oak tree by making it the gate, the entrance into the circle." Alain placed three broad stone steps below the oak, and two stone markers on either side. Then he established a long sinuous line in the form of a mown path from the driveway to the circle, and on each side punctuated the path with junipers, which, he says, grow wild on the nearby hills. A strip is kept mown around the outside of the circle to keep it visible. Otherwise, all around it is swaying field grass peppered with wild-flowers (cranesbills, euphorbias, poppies, pink and yellow vetch), gorse, and wild roses. Seeing this great pale circle, standing within it, one feels strangely moved. There is something magical about this artwork of Alain's, something so quiet and utterly simple, like a vast romantic gesture. "When you have a small budget and a big landscape, it is better to adapt the vegetation and then punctuate the space with stones, because stones are civilized and make a garden."

LEFT: *Helichrysum billows above a bench of Alain's, sculpted out of local stone and cement. For the armrests, he took an arch from the door of a dismantled bread kiln on the property, cut it into two pieces, and turned them upside-down.*

ABOVE: *Alain gathered the limestones scattered in his meadow and created a great ghostly circle. A curving path marked by junipers leads to the circle, which seems to celebrate its setting of field flowers, gorse, and wild roses.*

Alain loathes anything chic. This is a man with a deep visceral love of the land for its own sake, a man who thrills to the challenge of creating art with the simplest of available materials. He feels that the best artistic creations often emerge when money is limited. "Designers need restrictions," he says. In the garden, it forces you to be closer to the vernacular, to use what's there.

One day, Alain took me to Villeneuve les Avignon to see the garden he feels most influences him, in part to prove his point. L'Abbaye St. André is an elegant, terraced Italianate garden within the ramparts and remains of an ancient Benedictine abbey that looks across the Rhone to the Palace of the Popes in Avignon. Although open to the public, the garden is private, and without a big staff to maintain it, survives on a minimum of upkeep. Herein, Alain feels, lies much of its charm. Because there is no watering and no fussing, the plants in the garden have to survive on their own. Therefore, the plants of the *garrigue,* the vernacular plants of Provence, are relied on. Olives, cypress, iris, rosemary, santolina, sage, genista, broom—these are the plants that are used at L'Abbaye St. André because

they can stand the drought of summer. Alain loves the strong bones of this Italian garden, but what he mostly loves is its wildness. It has an exuberance that is Provence; it appeals because it is powerful, simple, rugged, and because it sustains itself and remains glorious without coddling.

A garden of Alain's near La Chabaude is a favorite project for some of the same reasons. ("I call it my little sweet," he says.) The owners, an American jazz pianist and his French wife, are often away traveling. As at the *abbaye*, there can be no watering; the garden has to fend for itself.

The site is spectacular, at the end of a narrow curving road—more of a dirt track—edged with genista and blue flax, high up a hillside. The old stone farmhouse is set against verdant cliffs from which the owners have a panoramic view across a valley to blue mountains and the medieval hill town of Saint Martin de Castillon. To a garden designer, a view like this is, in a sense, daunting. Truly, Alain explained, "there is no end to the garden." Realizing how very beautiful it was before he did anything, Alain was careful not to disturb that view. The land directly around the house, however, was ragged, even "a bit sinister-looking," when the

LEFT: *For clients with an old farmhouse and a spectacular view of a medieval town across the valley, Alain set a pool into the hillside. A terrace wall sweeps up the hill in a curve.*

ABOVE: *Alain fashioned an arbor out of old stone pillars and oak branches to frame a view of the hill town, Saint Martin de Castillon, in the distance.*

owners bought it in 1993. Alain terraced it with steps and walls, using clean, pure, contemporary lines of stone and gravel, then added cypress ("always a good plumb line," he points out) and herbs to accent and cushion his geometry. Steps through walled beds of iris and sage lead down from the blue-shuttered house to a new swimming pool set against the hillside. It will be screened from the house when a newly planted semicircle of cypress matures enough to knit together. A stone wall curves up the hillside above the pool, ending in one of Alain's signature stone benches, bordered with lavender "to echo the sky." Just below the pool, an *allée*

of olive trees, framed in squares of stone, signals the end of the cultivated garden. Beyond the olives, wild forest growth cascades down into the valley. The rugged simplicity of this garden deliberately echoes the landscape.

Alain had obvious fun creating an arbor ("the *conservatoire*," the amused owners call it) a short walk from the house. Old stone pillars mark the place, which was until recently a garbage dump. The owners wanted to raze the pillars, but Alain persuaded them to let him play with the spot. He fashioned an arbor by lacing oak branches between the pillars and planting grapes and honeysuckle to climb the structure. With some old red floor tiles he found stacked up in a corner, Alain made a mosaic pattern in cement on the ground beneath the arbor. Most of the tiles are set on edge, just slivers of color, interspersed with some squares in an exuberant sunburst he calls his "Jackson Pollock sundial." Again, he has delighted in using found objects to fashion a piece of art. The owners talk now of holding an *intime* concert at the *conservatoire*.

North of Apt, in a town near Mont Ventoux and a jagged mountain range called The Laces of Montmirail (Dentelles de Montmirail), a garden on a grander scale has absorbed much of Alain's creative energy for the last few years. Like so many Provence gardens, it is set on a hillside, on a series of terraces extending out and down from the town's handsome eighteenth-century

LEFT: *Beneath the arbor of oak branches and old stone pillars, Alain designed a floor mosaic out of roof tiles he found discarded in a corner of the property. The tiles are set in cement, some flat, most on end, in a sunburst pattern.*
RIGHT: *For a terrace outside a chateau near Mont Ventoux, Alain had iron chairs and a table made with maple and oak leaves in the design to reflect the favorite trees of the owners—one of whom is American, the other French.*

chateau. Alain has completely reworked the three main terraces, giving each a new, distinct personality.

Grand old lime trees shade an area paved with limestone squares just outside the house, where a table and chairs, designed by Alain, are arranged for eating and enjoying the splendid view across the garden to the mountains of "lace." When the owners bought the chateau in 1992, this highest terrace was closed in by yew hedges. Alain replaced the yew with iron railings, giving an airier, more expansive feeling. Then he sited a broken Roman column, which he discovered behind the chateau, at the far end of the terrace to establish a perspective. Beyond the column, huge cypresses interrupt the panorama of hills in the distance. Three iron trellises have been placed to the east, south, and west of the column, and together they symbolize for Alain the four points of the compass. Having positioned his "mineral" features, he added gently curving borders of perennials and shrubs. The color scheme here is limited to soft yellows, blue, and white—peaceful, says Alain, reflecting the sky.

A series of steps lead down to the middle terrace—which also possesses an extraordinary view—and the swimming pool. Here the color scheme is bolder, mostly orange and gold, always pleasing to see against the blue of water. Eight fruit trees in pots (orange and lemon) line one side of the pool between lengths of twisted railing Alain designed. On the opposite side, behind similar pots of boxwood, a high retaining wall is draped with orange flowering *bignon*. Heleniums, heliopsis, tangerine potentillas, teucrium, and erysimum grow along the base of the wall. Alain positioned a new pool house at one end of this terrace and balanced it with a massive seventeenth-century facade and fountain at the other end.

The third and lowest terrace is more intimate, and the theme is red fruit and flowers. A new iron pergola runs along the dividing wall of this garden, now draped with jasmine, white wisteria, and clematis. Clipped yew and santolina hedging has been planted in a maze-like pattern, in which strawberries, raspberries, currants, and red roses are growing. A limestone path leads to a small iris pool at one end, set in a mosaic of little

LEFT: *The chateau garden that Alain designed is on a series of terraces. The lowest terrace features a small iris pool at one end and an iron pergola planted with jasmine and clematis. To one side, a maze garden of yew is filled with red fruits and roses.*

ABOVE: *On the middle terrace of the chateau garden, the swimming pool is dominated by a seventeenth-century facade Alain found lying on*

the ground at a local stone merchant's. "It had been lying there for years; nobody knew how to use it." Pots of fruit trees line the terrace wall between lengths of iron railing Alain designed.

RIGHT: *A rill made of roof tiles directs spring water down a new allée of almond and fruit trees near the entrance to the chateau—and, Alain hopes, beckons visitors into the garden.*

stones. Alain thinks of these three terraces as representing three ages of life. This lowest terrace symbolizes birth and childhood—"red for the pain of coming out, a maze to play in, fishes, a little pool, *voilá!*" The middle terrace represents adulthood—strong color, bold architecture. The highest terrace is old age, broken a little (the antique column), with soft colors and serenity.

Alain always has a concept or a theme that explains how his gardens evolve, just as he does when he is creating a sculpture. Although Alain's garden near Mont Ventoux is grand in scope, befitting the chateau, its atmosphere is romantic, slightly wild, and bold. In addition, the plantings are appropriate to the setting. This is the first garden in which Alain used an extensive plant list. He relied on the knowledge of a nurseryman, Pierre Baud (an expert on figs), to help him devise it.

"What is wonderful about our profession," Alain says, "is that you meet someone who has a specialty and you share your expertise."

Alain has recently gone back to school to learn more about his new passion. He is working on his doctorate at L'École des Hautes Études in Paris in a newly-created department, the Philosophy of Landscape. "Because of my studies, I am thinking more and more about the landscape and how my garden, any garden, relates to it. Unless I have a walled garden—like jewelry in a box—I want to repeat the valleys and the hills. I think it is important to teach clients about the character of the territory, to make them sensitive to native plants, and to reveal to them the identity of the land they have bought. And it is important that everything we create has a meaning."

Steve Martino

Steve Martino

A MERICA IS IN DANGER OF BECOMING visually homogeneous, with the same plants—rarely native to where we live—jumbled together along streets and yards in yawning monotony. We grow plants, regardless of their origins, because we think they're pretty, or because our neighbors grow them, or they're what the nursery is pushing. We forget that they might have requirements that don't jibe with our own environment, and we often end up having to sustain them with great effort and energy. With no sense of place and no ethnicity, our gardens can be costly affairs. So it is heartening to know that in small but profound ways, designers like Steve Martino are bucking the trend.

Steve is quick to suggest that his own profession might be one of the problems. "Landscape architects are supposed to be the stewards of the environment," he says. But he wonders, "Would the land be better off if we were never there?" In many cases, he thinks, yes.

It is hard to distinguish the desert community of Phoenix, Arizona, where Steve lives and works, from a town in Florida or California. Emerald lawns, palms, orange trees, bougainvillea, oleanders, and pots of petunias fill front yards and back gardens. The lawns are irrigated (Phoenix gets seven inches of rain a year and at least ninety days of heat greater than one hundred), the palm trees are pruned of their shaggy beards (in Florida, this pruning process happens naturally), and the petunias look bizarrely out of place against the bumpy rust-red mountains of the Sonoran Desert. "These landscapes are like terminally ill patients," Steve laments. "It is a constant effort to keep them alive." Lawns alone, he says, require fifty inches of

PRECEDING PAGES: *A seemingly wild desert landscape is actually the front garden of a suburban home in Phoenix created by Steve Martino to harmonize with its natural surroundings.* LEFT: *Steve champions the use of native desert plants—until recently dismissed as weeds and unavailable at nurseries—in Arizona gardens. The silhouettes of the soaring saguaro cactus, wriggling ocotillo, and spiky agave are perfectly suited to the contemporary architecture and background of desert mountains seen around Phoenix, and give gardens there a vital sense of place.*

water a year to stay green. "Billions of dollars are spent to make Arizona look like something it's not."

As you drive along one particular road in the sprawling metropolis of Phoenix, on the left you will see startling green lawns beneath rows of groomed palm trees. On the right, where Steve's hand has been at work, you pass by bosks of graceful mesquite, silvery brittlebush, waving ocotillos, and the majestic saguaro cactus. How stunning, how perfect these desert plantings look. Slowly, the residents of Phoenix are learning to appreciate the sympathetic landscapes Steve has been championing for twenty years. And other landscape architects in Arizona are following his lead. "I've gone from heretic to hero," he likes to say, as he remarks on the rising demand for public and private gardens created with these easy-care natives. In the 1970s, no nursery sold indigenous trees, shrubs, and cactus—they were considered weeds. The desert was viewed as a wasteland and anything done to it as an improvement. Now, with a strong move toward regional ecology, native nurseries are flourishing.

Steve started using native plants in gardens as "a visual bridge," a way of connecting with the regional landscape. But he has discovered an unexpected bonus in his contrived desert landscapes over the years. As native plants are returned to the land, the indigenous pollinating insects are once again attracted, and with them the desert birds and other wildlife, like fox and havelina, a desert wild boar. "My gardens become habitats," Steve says. And his clients, enjoying the wildlife

brought to their gardens, become advocates of the desert ecology.

In a garden setting, these mixed desert plantings of Steve's not only teem with life but present stunning patterns. He is skilled at combining the plants of the desert to make the most of their beauty. (Cactuses stuck in the ground do not make a desert garden, according to Steve.) Feathery palo verdes are placed near spiky, whip-like ocotillos, plump brittlebush contrasts with soaring saguaros, bold-leaved agaves cluster with wispy penstemons and paddle-shaped opuntias. He loves the agaves and Mickey Mouse-like prickly pears for the drama of their silhouettes, and he plays their strong shapes and textures against the smooth sinuous walls and pools that are his other hallmarks. Steve believes that plantings are only half of garden design. The other half is hardscaping.

Steve approaches both aspects of his designs with the eye of an artist. "I think it's my work with black-and-white photography over the last thirty years that has helped me to see the importance of composition," he remarks. It is also his background in architecture that directs and inspires his work.

Halfway through architecture school, twenty years ago, Steve made a career change. Taking a break from school to earn some money after a motorcycle accident, he went to work for a landscape architect. He became quickly disgusted with the typical plantings of lawns, bougainvillea, and orange trees, and at the same time enthralled with the surrounding desert flora, or "weeds," that no one seemed to know much about. On a crusade to learn more about the desert natives, he started working with a local horticulturalist, Ron Gass, who shared his passion and knew the identity and sources of indigenous plants. This led to Steve's desire to create a new sort of garden embracing the desert. "I wanted to celebrate the desert, not make apologies for it."

"A landscape architect by chance" is how Steve described himself to a graduating class of landscape architects and planners at Arizona State University, where he accepted an award in 1996. Steve never had formal training, learning instead from observation and trial and error, and he feels it was to his advantage that he didn't know the rules and didn't have any preconceptions about his profession when he started designing gardens. On the other hand, he took advantage of the university's design library, and pored over books of ancient and contemporary gardens and architecture for inspiration. Moorish and Spanish gardens particularly impressed him, as well as the work of Luís Barragán and Franklin Israel.

"I am not a gardener," Steve told me stoutly, and perhaps a little defensively, knowing that I like to weed and muck about in the soil. What excites Steve is the process of designing walls, steps, pools, rills, fountains, and columns (like the architect he did not become), playing with their colors, curves, and configurations, then juxtaposing his plants against these structures, always with the desert in mind and the need there for shade and privacy.

A small garden he designed recently for Jay Hawkinson, a Phoenix resident, illustrates these priorities. The site is a narrow corner lot in a desert development in which all the facades of the houses and walls visible to the street are expected to be painted white. The appeal of this corner lot to its new owner was that it backed onto a drainage wash area, where, Steve notes, the richest gatherings of native desert plants are often found. An art director in downtown Phoenix, Jay Hawkinson wanted a refuge to come home to, one that was clean, spare, restful, yet colorful and inventive. After some research, he decided Steve Martino was his man.

At first, Steve addressed the back patio adjacent to the wash. Here, he was interested in the borrowed landscape, "visually taking ownership of the common desert open space" beyond the property line. He built a wall just high enough to screen the sidewalk from the house, but not high enough to obscure the desert

LEFT: *A small garden Steve designed as a refuge for a Phoenix art director offers vibrant color (the desert sun washes out all but the brightest colors), shade, and privacy on two levels of terrace. A yellow awning is stretched across an arc of magenta poles to shade a table and chairs within curves of lavender pink walls.* ABOVE: *A slender ocotillo, with orange-scarlet panicles of flowers, is set against plaster walls painted mauve and paper bag brown.*

plants. Then he added blue palo verdes and sweet acacia for shade, opuntia and aloes for pattern, and brittlebush, penstemons, and salvias for color. New steps leading down to the open space gave the appearance that the garden didn't end at the property line.

More recently, in a second phase of development, the long, wedge-shaped side yard has been transformed into the main garden area. Here, Steve and his client were more interested in a sense of containment and privacy, achieving a desired refuge from urban life. Steve created a sunken terrace by lowering the grade and adding long, simple concrete steps. Then he wrapped the terrace in a series of curved plaster walls (erasing all corners), creating a fountain and water channel as the focal point. The fountain, he notes, helps diminish traffic noise, and the curved walls focus the water's sound back to the patio. They also mask the existing development wall, which Steve finds "fussy," and allow him to play with color. Both Steve and his client love brilliant color and wanted to experiment with it. And, as Steve points out, the desert sun washes out colors and flattens them, and so there is a real need for boldness.

By adding different pigments to the cement plaster walls, Steve and Jay came up with a Matisse-like environment. The semi-circular sweep of wall that encompasses the terrace has been colored a mauvey lavender. This in turn is cut, down the main axis, by a terracotta-red wall curving around the end of the water channel. This combination of colors is made even more vivid in spring by a yellow-blooming palo verde arching just beyond the walls. A sliver of translucent neonred Plexiglas has been inserted in the red curved wall, ending this axis, and for added drama it is backlit at night. A sunflower-yellow awning stretched across an arc of magenta poles continues the curves of bright color and provides instant shade for a table and chairs. Across from the seating area, a small pyramid painted sapphire blue serves as a focal point of an axial view through the house into the garden.

Visiting the Hawkinson garden with Steve, I watched while he went through paint chips to decide on colors for the inside of the perimeter walls. For a length of wall to the right of the fountain he chose a vivid yellow, echoing a brittlebush in flower leaning

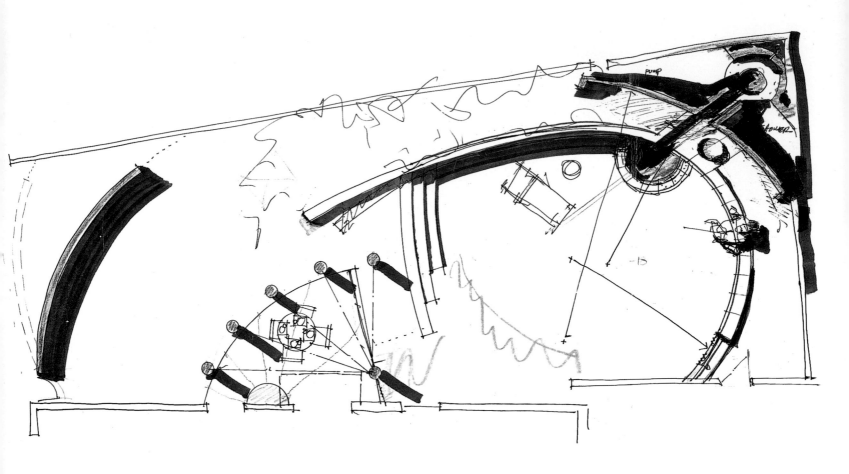

over it. For the opposite wall, he ended up having a brown paper bag scanned by a computer to serve as a model for the soft brown he wanted. It serves as a shadowy foil for the brilliant red penstemons and salvias and bold prickly pears scattered in front of it. The planting here, in a ground of decomposed gravel, is spare, but eventually, Steve says, the indigenous plants will grow until they are equal to the structure of the garden. He believes in letting his plantings go wild, "to wrack and ruin." Essentially, of course, what he wants is for his gardens to become naturalized, echoing the desert just outside the walls.

A certain amount of symbolism plays a part in Steve's designs. He likes to think about what his gardens look like from above, sketching the ground plane in patterns and shapes, and these configurations often take on symbolic meaning, evoking the spirit of the desert. A favorite shape that recurs in all Steve's work is the broken circle or arc, like the one used to define the terrace at Jay Hawkinson's. It reminds Steve of the ruins of the great kivas, ancient Indian stone structures,

sunken in the ground, that served as sacred meeting rooms. The fountain walls, if looked at from above, represent the figure of a man with open arms, and the water channel (his body) aligns with the axis of the sunrise on the summer solstice.

This particular solar symbolism was used once before by Steve for a land-art monument done in collaboration with the environmental artist Jody Pinto. Together they had won a design competition for a commission to create a boundary marker between the cities of Phoenix and Scottsdale that would also serve as a gateway to the adjacent Papago Park. Their goal was to address the park's dying ecology, to do something restorative as well as symbolic. The resulting monument, placed at the intersection of two highways, is a six-hundred-fifty-foot stone earthwork shaped like a tree of life. Each branch of the tree forms a terrace that catches water, and here Steve has seeded native palo verdes, brittlebush, ironweed, and cactus. His method harks back to old Indian irrigation practices in which rain water was harvested for crop production

LEFT: *Steve likes to work with the ground plane of his designs to develop patterns and shapes. The arc is a shape often repeated in his gardens, symbolizing for him the kivas in the desert, ancient cell-like Indian structures made of stone and sunken in the earth.* RIGHT: *The native brittlebush and a palo verde tree echo the color of a yellow wall when in flower.*

and survival. "The design is a functional farming and irrigation system that collects and distributes rain water. This time the crop is the desert itself."

A number of stone monoliths, built as vertical markers to break the skyline, cross the base of the tree of life and stretch on over a seven-hundred-foot expanse. With great care and some luck, Steve managed to align them with the sun on the summer solstice, "the longest farming day of the year." On June 21, at sunrise, the five mammoth pillars cast a straight line of shadows across the desert ground. For Steve, the Papago Park City Boundary is a monument to desert survival and regeneration. "The public was very responsive to this project: it seemed to fit a need for a sense of connection with the desert, its history, and its stewardship." Six hundred people showed up to help cast native seeds at City Boundary's dedication, held at sunrise on the summer solstice.

If City Boundary was a new and bold artistic interpretation for a busy city intersection, so in a way was Steve's planting scheme in 1991 for a courtyard at a corporate building in downtown Phoenix. The clients, owners of the progressive newspaper *New Times*, had decided to restore a derelict elementary school for their offices. They called Steve in to design something other than the typical Mediterranean-style landscape. Happy to prove that a native landscape was appropriate for urban corporate spaces, Steve planted regional desert trees to create a canopy of shade and a sense of enclosure on several levels of terrace. Rain water was collected in gullies and used to irrigate the plants. Now, lines of green-trunked palo verdes, sweet acacias, ironwood, and a bosk of mesquite cast patterned shadows around a green-tiled fountain, offering a picturesque oasis for city workers as well as giving them a sense of where they

live. Steve won an American Society of Landscape Architects award for his ecologically-sensitive design at *New Times,* and with his success helped generate interest in a regional approach to landscaping by other businesses.

The owner of *New Times* asked Steve recently to design the outdoor living spaces at his remodeled 1950s suburban hillside home. He wanted something appropriate for a young family—he and his wife have three little children—and he wanted a garden that served as a native plant habitat.

The site was governed by a hillside ordinance that forbade any new grading. A preexisting pool took up almost all of the backyard. Concrete walks, an asphalt drive, and non-native plants took up the rest.

With the residents' blessing, Steve promised to solve all their problems in the quirkiest way he could. He removed the pool and its accompanying deck to make

way for a large outdoor room. The hot, hard paving was replaced with decomposed granite. Then Steve wrapped the new garden room with an eight-foot-high, eighty-foot-long curving wall that retains and hides the awkward slope behind it, cleans up the view from the house, and gives the family some privacy. But this is no ordinary retaining wall: it not only curves, it tilts, in a startling fashion, away from the hillside and back toward the terrace and the house. Steve painted his canted wall a dazzling acid yellow, echoing the flower color of two palo verdes he planted by the house.

The work of the architect Franklin Israel, Steve says, inspired his yellow wall, although Israel's leaning walls and brilliant colors are confined to indoors. "His tree-less interior landscapes changed my life," Steve admits.

A cantilevered flight of concrete steps, stained dark gray, breaks through the yellow wall at one end of

the outdoor room, leading up the hillside to desert plantings of agaves and aloes, a picnic area, and a glorious view. The shadowy space beneath the steps offers a secret place for the children to play in. On the opposite side of the terrace, Steve built a long, asymmetrical, slightly curving concrete counter that looks something like a surfboard, which he painted green and set floating on a yellow pedestal. He incorporated a barbecue grill at one end of it, and surrounded it with shiny steel stools that have the appearance of flying saucers. When the children are older, he hopes they will climb onto those stools with their crayons and magic markers and use the counter as an art table.

The toddlers are already using a small fountain in the garden as a wading pool. Steve lined a simple circular pool with tiny iridescent green tiles, and notched it

ABOVE LEFT: *At the garden Steve designed for the owner of* New Times *and his family, a curved yellow wall conceals the trash bins. Another curved yellow wall, eighty feet long, serves as the backdrop to a terrace behind the house.*

TOP RIGHT: *Steve created a gate for the entrance drive using perforated steel fashioned into a series of sail-like panels.*

BOTTOM RIGHT: *Behind the house, Steve built a long curving concrete counter and lined it with shiny steel stools. A barbecue grill is set in one end of the table.*

into a low, broad concrete step by the house. For safety, he installed a removable stainless-steel screen which can be set one inch below the surface of the water.

Near the cantilevered stairs, a tall, green-stemmed ocotillo casts its wriggling shadow on the yellow wall. "Walls pick shadows up off the ground like magic," Steve says. The blue palo verde trees also create graceful silhouettes, and break the starkness of the terrace.

For night time, Steve has strung Italian Christmas lights across this outdoor room, which throw interesting shadows and add sparkle. The owners recently asked Steve to devise more shade for this garden room to protect the children against the brutal summer desert sun. After hours of research and cartooning, Steve came up with trelliswork in the form of "big kites, bat wings, as huge and as delicate as I could make them and still have them be safe. I think they will steal the show."

An intricate gate Steve designed for the entrance to the property is stealing the show already. A gate was needed across the driveway, but rather than devise a purely functional barrier, Steve went one step further and created a work of art. Using perforated steel, he fashioned a series of sail-like panels that bend (as though with the wind) and overlap, casting shadows against each other. They form an eerily transparent and delicate sliding screen. His creation, Steve says, is in the spirit of the Dragon Gate in Barcelona, designed by Antonio Gaudí. But Gaudí's gate is ornately decorated in art nouveau style; Steve's is unornamented.

As you walk through Steve's gate to the front entrance of the house, you pass a smaller, round version of the yellow garden wall. This smaller wall conceals the trash containers and purple-tinted prickly pears are highlighted against it. Several levels of steps and terraces lead you to the front door and a view of the seemingly wild desert landscape tumbling down the hillside. It has all been contrived by Steve to harmonize with the surrounding countryside.

Steve's goal is to bridge the gap between environmental responsibility and art, or what he calls "high design." Good design, he says, is free. It's about being willing to go beyond the ordinary.

PRECEDING PAGES: *The glassed living room of the house leads out to a front terrace and mirror-like reflecting pool embraced by the bold shapes and textures of desert planting.* LEFT: *Green-trunked palo verdes offer graceful silhouettes and ocotillos throw writhing shadows against a curved yellow wall.* RIGHT: *Steve enjoys playing textured plants, like paddle-shaped prickly pears and armored agaves, against the stark garden walls he creates. Plants are only half the story in gardens, Steve feels; equally important is the hardscaping—the walls, steps, pools, and fountains he loves to design.*

Ron Lutsko

*Ron*Lutsko

TRAVELING WITH RON LUTSKO through the hills that fringe San Francisco is an education in botany, ecology, and the historic effects of farming and modern technology on the California landscape. On jaunts in the lushness of early spring and the ripe golden days of autumn, Ron taught me about the microclimates of the coastal range, how, for instance, in Napa Valley, the hills facing east are rich in vegetation, whereas the western-facing hills are dry and comparatively barren. He taught me how to identify the four species of native oaks that have so much to do with the indigenous beauty of this part of California, and how they are indicators of the specific type of enviroment you are driving or walking through. He pointed out rows of shaggy eucalyptus trees, invasive foreigners that have become an important visual element in the landscape, valued as windbreaks even though they are only marginally hardy. We climbed up into serpentine, the dryest, leanest habitat for plants, characterized by iron-laden rock outcroppings and wildflowers as far as the eye can see—the "real California," Ron calls it, where only the native plants are able to survive. We hiked past red-stemmed, satin-smooth manzanitas, Ron's favorite native shrub, and gnarled, bonsai-like oaks to reach the hilltops, where carpets of poppies, goldfields, creamcups, and linanthus painted the rocky ground. "Originally, the whole state looked like this," Ron said, before the first Spaniards came up from Mexico bringing seed of foreign grasses with them in the fodder for their cattle. Eventually, the grasses became invasive, spreading thickly in the richer swales of the hills and choking out the less assertive native grasses and wildflowers.

PRECEDING PAGES: *Ron Lutsko enjoys juxtaposing grids of plants against rolling topography, as he does here with an orchard of lavender on a ranch south of the Bay area.* **LEFT**: *For inspiration, Ron explores the mountainous rock-strewn landscape called serpentine, where wildflowers native to California still carpet the ground.* **RIGHT**: *In this Lutsko garden south of San Francisco, boldly patterned lines of herbs give way to naturalistic sweeps of goldfields* (Lasthenia glabrata) *and bunchgrass under oak trees, echoing the surrounding natural landscape.*

Ron's idea of bliss is being alone with nature—hiking, fly fishing, exploring in the wilderness—whether in the mountains of California or north into Alaska—and seed collecting just about anywhere. With his colleague, Wayne Roderick, he publishes a seed list of bulbs and herbaceous plants that are mostly alpine rarities. He is passionate and knowledgeable about his native California flora, and fascinated by the variable topographical conditions that allow different plants to flourish in contiguous but contrasting habitats. As an example of this, he drove me from the rich riparian valley of Napa to the interior of the bordering hills, dark and lush with pines and ferns; then out onto steeply rolling dry meadows dotted with blue oaks, their trunks silver with lichens; and finally to rugged, wild, flower-strewn serpentine—all within a period of minutes. The climate of coastal California is basically Mediterranean, with dry, hot summers and wet, mild winters. But the ocean and mountain ranges of the Bay area often intensify the climate, causing unexpected variables (like fog in the city), which Ron says make designing gardens there more interesting and more fun.

At the University of California campuses at Berkeley and at Davis, Ron received degrees first in horticulture and then in landscape architecture in 1980. Now, he takes time out from his landscape architecture practice to teach planting design to students at both Davis and Berkeley. I suspect these college students are as stirred by his ebullient enthusiasm, passion for the enviroment, and encyclopedic knowledge of plants as I was on our excursions through the coastal countryside.

LEFT: *Ron's backyard, in Lafayette, California, holds his own private nursery of plants raised from seeds and cuttings.* ABOVE: *California natives wildly flourish in the middle of San Francisco at the Arthur Menzies Garden in the Strybing Arboretum. Ron says he would design the garden differently today—in grids perhaps, like the streets of the city.*

Ron first won public acclaim for his sensitive redesigning and replanting of the Arthur Menzies Garden of California Native Plants at the Strybing Arboretum in San Francisco in 1990. It is amazing to walk along his paths, in the middle of the city, among explosions of meadow flowers—yellow mimulus, blue Douglas iris and gilias, bunchgrasses, and white foamflower. Seven thousand native plants are represented here, half of them found only in California, but you don't feel like you're walking through a botanical display. Although the various parts of the garden are planted to resemble different wild habitats (Ron has done this more recently at the University of California Botanical Garden in Berkeley), the whole is planted so artistically, with such sweeps of plants, that you feel, more than anything, that you are wandering through a particularly beautiful wild garden.

Ron says he would design it differently today. Although he admits that the natural wildness of this city garden offers a wonderful surprise and respite, he feels it is not "of the place," that it should perhaps do more to acknowledge its surroundings. "I think I would do an

urban interpretation," Ron says, planting in grids, maybe, to suggest city streets. "People think that native plants should be used in natural configurations. But all plants are native somewhere. Why not plant them in patterns?"

Ron is a modernist at heart. Although he says, ruefully, that "modernism and technology are unifying the world in a way that is erasing local culture," and he believes strongly that we mustn't let this happen, nevertheless he enjoys seeing the hand of man in nature. He speaks fondly of the absurdity of the Jeffersonian grid system imposed on the streets of San Francisco, with its impossibly rolling terrain. He thrills to the linear patterns of the vineyards, dramatically juxtaposed against the mountains in wine country, bringing "a human perspective" to this imposing landscape. He prefers to show, not hide, the infrastructures in his gardens, thinking of them as our connection with nature.

Ron follows in the footsteps of octogenarian Dan Kiley, one of America's most eminent landscape archi-

tects, who believes that gardens should be outright reflections of the hand of man, not artificial imitations of nature: "It's not man and nature. It's not even man with nature. Man is nature, just like the trees." Educated in the Bauhaus tradition of modernism, Kiley nevertheless turned away from the asymmetrical garden design favored by his colleagues Thomas Church and Garrett Eckbo in California, returning instead to formal geometry and classical axial views to create his own modernist gardens. Brushing aside design theories, Kiley speaks of the strong influence of functional land use in his work. "All farmland is beautiful, and orchards, the way fields are cut. That's real landscape design, dynamic and exciting—a natural intersection of man and the earth."

In the same spirit, Ron takes the grids of city streets and the lines of the vineyards and incorporates them into his designs. The concepts of his designs are born out of the sites themselves, how he sees them, and what they mean to him. He stresses the importance of the surrounding landscape to the makeup of his gardens. "If you pay close enough attention to the site, the design of the garden is already there."

Ron calls the garden he designed at a cattle ranch south of the Bay area "dead simple," but a great deal of thought and inspiration went into its creation. As we approached this garden in spring through rolling green hills and serpentine outcroppings covered with wildflowers, I felt we could just as well have been in the Irish or English countryside. But Ron was quick to remind me that this same landscape would look more like Jerusalem come summer. Drought, intense summer heat, and a poor, stony soil were factors that made the selection of tough, drought-tolerant plants for this garden imperative. Ron also chose plants that he felt reflected the texture, colors, and forms occurring in the surrounding landscape.

The garden was designed in layers, Ron explained, a series of transitions between the architecture of the house and the distant landscape. Closest to the low-slung farmhouse, Ron placed a simple rectangular bed that he planted with a row of manzanitas and "a solid field" of white fleabane. The geometric mass of flowers relates to the architecture of the house, but is interrupted by a natural stone outcropping that Ron deliberately left intact. Here he planted a carpet of woolly thyme and underplanted it with native bulbs and annuals. He thinks of this first "level" of his design as the most "gardenesque," consisting of cultivated garden flowers, which seemed appropriate just next to the house. From here, a panel of lawn leads the eye toward the distant view. Its edges are "not crisply defined, but rather shaped by the random pattern of the stones that form the surrounding walks." Ron's notched lawn edges were meant to illustrate how the geometry of his design begins to erode, to be eaten away, as you walk away from the

LEFT: *A sandstone path, leading away from the ranch house in this rural garden, is randomly notched into a rectangular panel of lawn, thereby "eating away" the strict geometry of Ron's design. Beyond, rows of rounded lavender lead your eye out to the rolling hills.*
RIGHT: *The plan shows the series of transitions from formal to informal structure as Ron connects the garden to the natural landscape.*

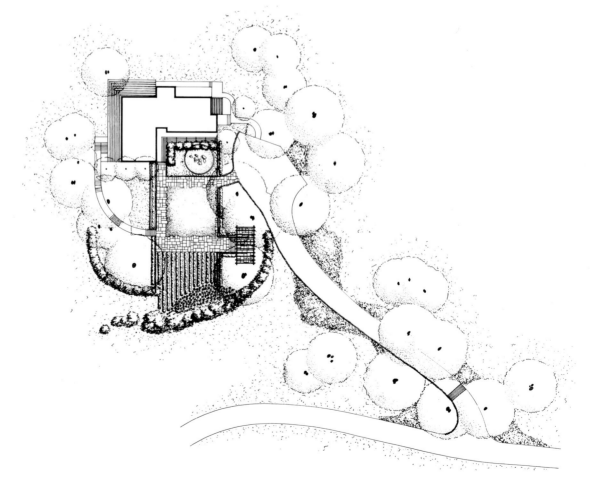

house. The sandstone he used for the paving is the same red color of the region's soil, and has a rippled pattern to it reminiscent of water—a pleasant suggestion in a dry garden.

Beyond the lawn, grids of lavender take the design another step away from architecture, at the same time leading your eye to the distant hills. Ron thinks of the lavender as having the structural integrity of stone in a softer medium. Lavender relates to the surrounding chaparral in habit—gray and scrubby—and, in Ron's planting pattern, it is a reference to the agricultural heritage of the area, where orchards once thrived.

The last layer of planting consists of a curve of manzanita defining the edges of the garden. "At the central axis of the view the arc erodes into an informal mass of manzanita that reaches out to the natural landscape." Manzanitas are the predominant native shrub of the site, and, to Ron, are one of the "true icons" of the California countryside.

Ron planted a slope shaded by oaks on one side of the garden with a brilliant carpet of native goldfields (*Lasthenia glabrata*), white and purple linanthus, and bunchgrasses (*Festuca californica*). Vast sweeps of Spanish lavender (*Lavendula stoechas*), which, Ron says, seeds around here in the dry earth, are planted in naturalistic waves along the drive, and combined with California fuschia (*Epilobium californica*), a dramatic white poppy aptly called the fried egg plant (*Romnyea Coul-*

teri), and other native flowers below the garden proper. Ron encouraged the flowers to naturalize into the fields where they thrive without extra care or watering.

Venerable blue oaks, indigenous to the site, give stature to the garden, and are echoed by an arbor Ron built out of copper columns that have developed a patina of the same hue as the lichen-covered trunks of the oaks. Originally Ron planted rue beneath the oaks to mirror their blue color. But the rue failed to thrive and it has been replaced with sculptural mounds of santolina.

Visiting this garden recently, Ron was upset to discover that a large planting of bunchgrass, *Stipa gigantea,* had been removed in his absence. He had planted the grass, with its mounded shape and warm buff flower heads, to mimic the golden California hills. "Those hills and that *stipa* really worked," he said, missing their visual play in the garden. "Plants can have a more important role than how they play as a composition. They can portray a thought. The *stipa* was part of the bigger composition and concept." The inevitable frustration of designing other people's gardens is seeing one's vision changed. This is why the great Russell Page

was reluctant to have the gardens he designed photographed years later. He knew his gardens rarely remained as he had envisioned them.

On the other hand, it is often a pleasure for a designer to have clients who enjoy tending a garden themselves and consequently take an active role in its development. This was the case when Ron designed a small backyard property for clients in Lafayette, California. Their house is low and Mediterranean-looking, very open to the outdoors, with an indoor pool at one end of the living room that continues outside beyond

the windowed walls into the garden. "We wanted to find a way to pull the water all the way back to the end of the garden," Ron explains, and indeed the main view from the house leads across the uncluttered, rectangular outdoor pool to an arched arbor, repeating the arches of the living-room windows, and beyond to a water basin and fountain at the end of the axis.

The clients wanted formality in their garden, but not necessarily a traditional design. Ron created for them what he calls "a modern classical garden." "It was done on a shoestring," he adds proudly. "There was no

PRECEDING PAGES: *Spanish lavender* (Lavendula stoechas), *in dazzling flower in May, tumbles onto the driveway. Ron describes the site of this garden in ranch country as "a little paradise."* ABOVE LEFT *and* LEFT: *Clients of Ron's in Lafayette, California, wanted a formal—but not necessarily traditional—garden in their small backyard. The result is a spare design of pool and terrace bordered with a checkerboard pattern of herbs. Industrial steel was used for arbors, gates, and fencing, and allowed to rust to a mellow red color.* ABOVE RIGHT: *A charming double flower border is hidden from view behind the fence along one length of the central garden.*

budget for expensive details." The arbor, which is a central feature of the garden, is spare in design, made of inexpensive tubular steel that has been allowed to rust to a dull red. It is a pleasing contrast to the blue of the pool and its pale stone perimeter. The same rusted steel was fashioned into a fence enclosing the garden. At the foot of the fence, blue oat grass in strict rows edges a planting of pale blue sage (*Salvia uliginosa*), which blooms all summer. On either side of the arbor, Ron set green santolina and lavender in a trim, checkerboard pattern, simple diagonal grids of "green, gray, green." Beyond the fence on one side, hidden from the main part of the garden, an arbor-covered walk, bound by colorful flower borders, extends from a small private terrace to a bench at the property line. Here, the wife indulges her love of gardening. The surprise of this intimate profusion of flowers is especially pleasing after the formality and streamlined geometry of the central space.

One of Ron's more complex garden designs blends both public and private garden space at a nineteenth-century winery in the Napa Valley. The main building, built of stone, with a new contemporary addition, serves as a residence for its owner as well as gallery space and an office for a private foundation that funds the arts. Several other buldings—a concrete shed, a winery, a garage, and a pool-house—existed on the property when Ron was first approached about designing the landscape. The site "looked like a freeway construction zone," he said.

Ron's challenge was to knit together the disparate buildings, connecting the outdoor spaces, at the same time allowing each area to have its own personality. He wanted the garden "to be about the place it is in," the riparian corridor of the Napa River, with its geometric-patterned valley of vineyards. He used the straightforward construction materials of the old winery—concrete and steel—for his designs, emphasizing his belief in "living with, not hiding, the apparatus of our modern age." Common tubular steel structures, echoing the fences and supports in the vineyards, were used throughout the garden for arbors, gates, and stairs. He designed runnels of water out of concrete to lead from one area of the garden to the next, tying the various parts of the garden together and, at the same time, symbolizing the canals and irrigation ditches in the vineyards. Limestone bands, set in stone dust, were used to mimic and enhance the water channels along the walkways.

Water was used in other ways—spilling in sheets down metal shades on a wall to buffer noise near the public entry, dripping gently into a fountain near the entrance to the residence, and falling from a pipe near

ABOVE: *White-flowering redbuds,* Cercis canadensis *'Alba', are planted in a row in paving, at the entrance to a Lutsko garden in Napa Valley.* LEFT: *The narrow concrete channel of water helps to knit together the disparate elements of this old vineyard property, which now houses an arts foundation as well as a private home.* RIGHT: *The wheelchair entrance to the gallery curves past a stone sculpture by Andy Goldsworthy. Valley oaks and Italian cypresses play against the horizontal lines of a privet hedge and the stone dust courtyard.*

the metal shed of the winery into a canal that disappears under the driveway and reappears in a garden courtyard.

Pleached magnolias forming a pergola, a row of redbuds against a blue wall, a linear grid of olives and robinias around a pool, and vines and rambler roses entwining the ironwork all offer patterned shade in the relentless summer heat. Ron combined garden plants common in the area with the region's drought-tolerant natives—iris, grasses, and herbs—in spare, uncomplicated plantings. The resulting garden has an understated, contemporary, linear design that retains the simplicity of functional farmland, soothes with water and shade, pleases the eye with pattern, and speaks of its surroundings.

"You have to think and think to get something simple," Ron says with typical straightforward modesty. I know how easy it is to clutter up a garden, lose sight of a concept, and fail to tie the different parts into a whole. Ron's gardens have a unifying theme or idea that makes them work visually as well as conceptually. They succeed, too, because of his flair for filling spaces with chaste linear patterns, created with a sensitive choice of hard materials (stone, gravel, iron) and plants he knows to be appropriate to the environment. His gardens are testaments to his abiding passion for his native landscape and an acknowledgement of man's never-ending manipulation of that landscape.

LEFT: *In a herbaceous border behind the olive trees that surround the pool, Ron planned a succession of perennials to create single bands of color. Hellebores are followed by euphorbias; later, irises are succeeded by lady's mantle, and, finally, sky blue* Salvia uliginosa. ABOVE: *Ron's water treatments often appear as delightful surprises, as with this gently dripping fountain edged by ferns. The walls are lined with white-flowering coralbells.* RIGHT: *Creating shade was important in this hot Napa valley garden. Olive trees are underplanted with lime green helichrysum and bearded iris.*

Nancy McCabe

Nancy McCabe

"I ALWAYS WANTED TO GROW the flowers in Dutch flower paintings," Nancy McCabe said as I was admiring some striped tulips and hose-in-hose primroses she had planted. Indeed, the exquisite bulbs and perennials that appear over and over in her gardens seem to have been plucked right out of a seventeenth-century botanical painting.

Nancy's background is in art, having studied first at the Maryland Institute of Art in Baltimore and then at the Minneapolis Art School. It was during this period that she fell in love with Dutch floral art and also became fascinated by the Renaissance lunettes depicting the Medici villas. "My interest was always in painting, sculpture, and art history. I got into garden design by accident."

Nancy grew up gardening in Macon, Georgia. Her father loved to garden, and employed Nancy and her three siblings to help with the weeding ("It was slave labor"). She still speaks of a fondness for the camellias and magnolias that flourished there. In Minneapolis, Nancy lived in an apartment with a front yard, where she cultivated her first garden: "I dug it with soup spoons and grew spinach and marigolds." Other gardens followed as she moved around the east and remained involved in sculpture and painting. Gradually, she realized she wanted to work out-of-doors full-time.

Creating a garden for her future husband in front of his bookstore in Salisbury, Connecticut—she had met him while she was buying garden books there—was a turning point in 1980 and the beginning of her career. The tiny garden of perennials surrounding a brick path to a bench, all overhung by a strangely clipped scented

PRECEDING PAGES: *A cutting garden, tucked away from the house on a rural Connecticut property, is enclosed by a fanciful twig and wire fence that keeps out the deer.* LEFT: *In a picturesque landscape in Kent, Connecticut, Nancy McCabe's bridge, railed with locust twigs, spans a stream on a walk from an old pool to an orchard path. "I don't like things that are so pure they don't have a quirkiness to them," Nancy says, explaining some of her unexpected rustic touches.* RIGHT: *Nancy designed a series of wooden supports for shrub roses that are underplanted simply with lady's mantle (Alchemilla mollis).*

magnolia, was admired by a well-known interior designer who lived nearby. "He grilled me for six months," Nancy recalled, then hired her to help him with his garden, which covered many acres of field and woodland. Nancy worked on that first project for six years, and with its success other commissions followed.

Most of Nancy's designing is concentrated in this northwestern corner of Connecticut, characterized by open, rolling farmland, rocky oak and maple woodland, fast-running streams, and picturesque villages of eighteenth- and nineteenth-century clapboard farmhouses clustered around a green. Nancy is always stressing the sense of place, the importance of making gardens that are appropriate to the houses they surround, and in this she succeeds brilliantly. Restraint and a lack of pretension in her designs, together with light touches of humor and whimsy, echo the straightforward air and individual charm of these New England farms and villages.

A hallmark of Nancy's work is the quality and refinement of her details. Even the smallest aspect of a garden is thought out, carefully arranged, and beautifully depicted. Although she never loses sight of the big picture, landscaping in bold strokes with groupings of one tree or a strong mass of complementary shrubs and sheets of ground cover, she always draws you into her gardens by creating intimate pictures as well. For example, a handcrafted clay pot of fragrant jasmine may

catch your eye, perched against a house wall on the side of a stone trough, the pink-budded star-like flowers spilling down to the place where water collects from a dripping spout. Or you may be entranced by tall crimson dahlias and tiny purple-striped morning glories trained up a tent-like chicken coop made of wire and painted wood and full of strutting bantam roosters and hens. Often, a slight quirkiness is revealed in her details, like the old garden chair that sits in her chicken pen (for whom?), and you know she is having fun. Always, too, some part of the garden is enclosed, private, and personal, a place where Nancy can indulge her talent for mixing the homely flowers, herbs, and vegetables she loves in satisfying rows and patterns. In this she is much influenced by kitchen gardens in France, from the magnificent Potager de Roi at Versailles to private working gardens she has glimpsed from the road.

Nancy is a master at using pots in gardens, filling them with often astonishing subjects, like sweet peas climbing up a five-foot tripod of woven sticks, or dusty pink boltonia thrusting through waving stalks of purple *Verbena bonariensis*. The pots themselves are as important to her as their contents, and she searches out appealing old clay and pottery on her travels through Europe and the United States. Often, she will cluster them together or line them on a bench or shelf, repeating the same plant—fringed striped pinks, perhaps, or

Ruby dahlias and tiny purple-striped morning glories clamber up the elegant pavilion Nancy designed for her chickens.
RIGHT: *Along the entrance path in the Kent, Connecticut, garden, fritillarias and grape hyacinths are liberally scattered in a groundcover of myrtle.*

golden-eyed auriculas—in similar pots. It is almost as though she were creating small paintings, still lifes for your eye to rest on at each turn. Chasteness and a delight in details, two seemingly disparate qualities, are smoothly, and imperceptibly, wedded in Nancy's style.

All the elements of her design style are evident in the landscaping she undertook for clients in South Kent, Connecticut. The house, a renovated nineteenth-century clapboard farmhouse sitting close by a winding country road, backed onto a picturesque landscape of sloping meadows and a stream. Dealing first with the ground directly around the farmhouse, Nancy erased a lot of "fussy planting." Her first instinct, as always, was to simplify. She had a low dry wall of local granite built to divide the house entrance from the adjacent drive-way, then planted a continuous sheet of myrtle on either side of a stone path from the driveway to the front door, where several plump bushes of boxwood were appropriately clustered—simple, clean, and unpretentious. But then Nancy added a fillip that gives the entrance a singular charm that is typical of her

work. In the myrtle, she tucked hundreds of delicate checkered fritillarias in mauve and white intermingled with small blue and white grape hyacinths. The bulbs bloom for maybe a week or two in May, a fleeting tapestry so memorable, so exquisite, that the plainness of the myrtle during the rest of the year is only seemly.

Nancy did more clearing below the barn, which nestles close to the house. Existing shrubs were cleaned up and underplanted with masses of a single variety of hosta for a unifying and striking effect. "I love the land here, the way it falls away from the house," Nancy said as we stood below the terrace walls on lawn that sweeps down into a field and an orchard. Nancy want-ed to line a path through the apple orchard with mag-nolias, echoing a handsome specimen by the barn, "something a little more unusual" than the crab apples her clients chose instead. In spring, thousands of white daffodils bloom among the fruit trees. "I do daffodils a lot for people," Nancy says, a feature that, along with her trademark orchards, is beautifully suitable to the New England countryside.

Nancy's borders of flowers were made to be savored up close, such as the gray garden you step down to at the foot of the terrace wall, where silver-leaved herbs and shrubs mix with white and mauve-pink blooms, repeating the colors of the saucer magnolia overhead. Tucked out of view beyond the barn lies one of Nancy's specialties—an intimate patterned cutting garden enclosed by a rustic twig fence. It was terraced with dry walls ("Stone walls work better in this climate when they're dry"—built without cement, Nancy said), creating two levels to deal with the sloping grade. The lower section was cut into a series of rectangular beds by a cobblestone path interrupted here and there by grist millstones "to funk it up." The beds in spring are neatly geometric, with rows of tulips, peonies, and leucojum to pick for bouquets. Annuals succeed the bulbs, and, by late summer, the garden has a blowsy, relaxed air. On the upper level, Nancy has covered the ground with stones interplanted with creeping herbs, creating what she calls a carpet garden. A wooden bench of her design, faded gray, sits at the end of the main path, and a pattern of semi-dwarf apple trees stands on each side, in stone-edged squares planted with maiden pinks (*Dianthus deltoides*). The twig fencing around the garden supports and camouflages wire required to keep out the deer. In summer it is draped with clematis, morning glories, and passion-flowers. Hardware cloth was added to the lower part of the fence and sunk into the ground to discourage rabbits and woodchucks. Originally, pinecones dangled like tassels from the open fretwork of the twig fence, but after a few years they rotted and were not replaced.

The rest of the garden was deliberately kept simple. Ferns are massed casually on a hillside as you walk to the stream, borders of lilacs screen an old pool, a rustic bridge made of locust branches leads to a mowed path up through meadow and orchard. "Things can get too complex," Nancy said. It is best, she feels, for a

design to be "simple and pure, to keep your complexity in one area." Gardens tend to get "too done," she added, when clients have a lot of money. Restraint—exquisitely evident in Nancy's gardens—"is the hardest thing to achieve."

One large-scale garden Nancy developed over a period of fourteen years, which in less sensitive hands might have turned into a nightmare of pretension, shows how restrained and personal her style is. The rather grand 1920s house, set high on a hill in open farmland, is neo-Georgian in style, of white-washed brick. It has "a very flat look" that Nancy loves, reminding her of two favorite houses down south: the William Paca House in Maryland and Stratford Hall in Virginia. To enhance that look, Nancy had a portico taken off the front of the house ("it was awful"), replacing it with bold stone steps and a gravel courtyard enclosed with curved brick walls to match the house. Italian clay pots of fragrant flowers in blue and white are staged along the steps, and the walls are traced with climbing hydrangea. A shadowy *allée* of limes leads from the curved entrance drive to the courtyard. To ease a drainage problem caused by the sloping grade, she had her favorite stonemason fashion an elegant line of gutters out of granite, similar to ones she had seen in Italy.

Behind the impressively sprawling house, Nancy built a high brick walled garden that, from the outside, appears equal to the house in size and scale. Inside, however, she divided the space into four separate gardens, thus creating an unexpected atmosphere of intimacy. Through an arched wooden door, you enter the first garden to discover a romantic profusion of perennials and shrubs in hues of purple, pink, white, and lavender. The colors, Nancy says, were dictated by a huge copper beech that weeps over one side of the garden wall. A side door leads down several steps into the next garden, which is quiet and plain in comparison:

Nancy concealed a series of intimate gardens within a high brick wall she designed to echo the scale and style of the house. **TOP LEFT:** *Through an arched wooden gate, you enter a romantic perennial garden, where a lavish tangle of sweet-scented flowers in mauve, purple, pink, and white are overhung by an ancient copper beech.* **BOTTOM LEFT:** *Down a few steps, you come to a much simpler garden where decorative paths of cut granite divide beds of swamp azaleas and ajuga. Fragrant magnolias and viburnums are espaliered against the walls.*

Japanese tree lilacs sit in a pattern on either side of a granite pathway that is bordered by rills, also of granite. Fragrant white-flowering shrubs have been espaliered aganist the walls. "It is just about water, and white," Nancy says, and sweet scents in the air. A few steps down again and you are in another garden, this one of swamp azaleas underplanted with ajuga. Following the granite path, you descend into the final garden, which is the most dramatic, with a strongly patterned paving of brick-edged granite squares surrounded by

TOP RIGHT: *A luxurious garden of gray foliage and white flowers, strikingly juxtaposed against a patterned floor of brick and granite, is the final destination within the high brick wall.*

BOTTOM RIGHT: *Fragrant white acidanthera, blue petunias, heliotrope, and scaevola are staged in pots along the entrance steps of this neo-Georgian house. The owner's favorite color is deep blue.*

pots and beds of white flowers and gray-leaved plants. In one corner, a romantic brick tower, hinting of Sissinghurst, serves as a toolshed. It rises two stories above the garden, giving the outside wall some needed height and balance where it dips with the sloping grade.

Nancy's favorite part of this grand project is a greenhouse and kitchen garden she designed some distance from the house. Although the greenhouse is vast, extending out in two wings from a central potting room, once inside you are struck by how friendly it seems, and

you realize you are being charmed by Nancy's composition. Old bricks set simply in stone dust in an appealing herringbone pattern line the floor, where clay pots of passionflowers and jasmines are gathered. White-painted tables run down the eastern length for smaller pots of herbs and tiny-flowered fuchsias. The old dark wood of the potting room comes as a visual relief after the brilliant light of the glass-enclosed wings, and, with Dutch doors letting in fresh air on two sides, must be a pleas-

THIS PAGE: *A newly planted orchard and greenhouse, planned down to the pots by Nancy, are set dramatically in the rolling farmland of New York State.* TOP RIGHT: *Nancy's own greenhouse was built by her husband Mike with cedar salvaged from a similar structure that was being torn down. In its angle, an intimate terrace area is arranged for alfresco meals, enhanced by pots of sweet-smelling flowers.* BOTTOM RIGHT: *A bold planting of oakleaf hydrangeas masks one side of a small vegetable garden, which is fenced with a pattern of twigs.*

ant place to work. Nancy designed every particular, even selecting the clay pots, and did the original drawings of the construction, after which she had an architect do the working drawings. A large kitchen garden stretches out behind the greenhouse, hedged in on three sides by lines of hornbeam. Dirt paths divide the beds, where rows of vegetables and flowers are staked and mulched with salt hay. The idea, Nancy said, was to keep this working garden as plain as possible.

Nancy's own greenhouse and kitchen garden are scaled-down versions of her designs for clients. They are also intensely personal expressions of what she cares about in a garden, containing the well-used tools and pots she loves and her favorite plants, arranged in thoughtful, whimsical vignettes. The first thing you see as you drive up to Nancy's house is a high lacy hedge of espaliered apple trees and, beyond it, glimpses of brick paths through rows of herbs and vegetables. The small beds, edged with glossy brown scalloped tiles Nancy found in Savannah, Georgia, are planted seasonally—

ABOVE TOP: *From Nancy
McCabe's driveway, you reach
the kitchen door by walking
through an entrancing* potager
*enclosed by espaliered apples
and a clipped hemlock hedge.
"I love fruit trees," Nancy admits,*
"especially espaliered ones."
ABOVE BOTTOM: *Striped
tulips dress her kitchen beds in
May.* RIGHT: *Nancy terraced
her steeply sloping back yard
with a simple stucco retaining
wall about five feet high,*
*capped with painted wood
boards. Terracing it twice
would have been too fussy,
she decided. Steps lead down
into a flower garden where
a small stone trough holds
water for birds.*

lettuces and striped tulips in spring, lavender and Madonna lilies in June, dahlias, onions, parsley, and cabbages in summer. Bricks and thyme, arranged in a quirky zigzag pattern, edge the main path to the kitchen door. Italian clay pots and old glazed jars from France billow with great bosomy hydrangeas or delicate jasmines. Tin and copper watering cans, green with age, and glass cloches add an old-world air to Nancy's *potager*, but they are more than picturesque. The cans are used for quick watering, the cloches to protect

spring seedlings from sudden frosts. "I love simple old garden things," Nancy says, "but I think they should be used for their intended purposes."

The same sort of straightforward appeal convinced Nancy to buy her present home. "The house was mighty plain," she says with just a hint of a southern drawl, "and I loved that." Sited squarely on a back road that leads to a canal at the foot of the Berkshires, it is an oddity for New England, built of stucco rather than of clapboard or shingle. It reminded Nancy of farmhouses

Fritillaria persica, pheasant's eye narcissus, grape hyacinths, and primroses flower beneath the trees and along paths in a stretch of woodland behind Nancy's house. Tringa, a chocolate Labrador retriever (along with Nell, a Norfolk terrier, and Polly, a Westie) keeps Nancy company in the garden.

in France, and she was entranced to think she could grow vines up its sides (not practical to do with a typical painted wooden house). She trained wisteria over the dark green windows and front door, and planted three espaliered pears to break the starkness of the facade on the road side. With old cypress struts rescued from a demolition, Nancy's husband built a small greenhouse adjoining the kitchen at the back of the house. A stone terrace now nestles into the resulting corner, where Nancy clusters more herbs and fragrant bulbs in pots around a weathered teak table and chairs. Beyond the terrace, on ground that slopes sharply away from the house, Nancy built a stucco retaining wall in order to level a square area below for a perennial garden. The wall is capped with board, painted dark green, and wooden steps ("a lot less expensive than stone") descend into the garden. The lower sides of the garden are enclosed by an unadorned board fence, also painted dark green. "I am not crazy about fussy things," Nancy said by way of explanation. She knew, too, that the stucco wall, wooden stairs, and plain fence would be in keeping with the spare style of the house.

Nancy says her favorite area of her garden,

besides the *potager*, is the patch of woodland she is working on. In a simple ground cover of myrtle, she has planted varieties of pale yellow primulas, many harking back to those Dutch floral portraits, yellow-brown perennial foxgloves (*Digitalis ferruginea*), and masses of fritillarias and poet's narcissus. Hellebores, favorites of Nancy's, are planted in patches in the myrtle, too, which is used around shrubs and beneath trees as a common denominator, visually tying together separate plant elements. "People don't understand that you need simplicity to be lavish." Nancy always seems to know when to stop, when to refrain from adding yet another sort of plant, and this restraint inevitably results in a pleasing visual impact. She will limit herself to one color, for example, in a mixed shrubbery—white buddleias with white rose of Sharon—or tie a planting together with one ground cover, such as vinca, violets (sometimes a pale variety called 'Freckles'), or woolly thyme. But then she will add some distinct note, some eccentric touch, to remind you that this is not a park but rather a very private creation.

Nancy loves animals—birds, dogs, and chickens in particular—and she enjoys designing housing for them to

ornament her garden and the gardens of clients. In a shaded spot at the end of an axis below her perennial garden, Nancy placed a tiered birdhouse that resembles the tower of Pisa. For a friend's Norfolk terriers, she designed a Gothic doghouse, and for another client, a rococo cathouse. In collaboration with a local cabinetmaker, she fashions benches, seats, and tables for her clients' gardens, often in chinoiserie, painted sober colors or allowed to weather. She designs with a sense of fun and an unfailing eye for the appropriateness of her ornaments.

Nancy finds one of her current projects, developing a garden for a well-known contemporary artist who lives in nearby Sharon, Connecticut, particularly refreshing. Striving for a look sympathetic with his style, she first addressed a courtyard area made by the two wings of his large, shingled Edwardian studio. She placed long granite stones by the center doorway to be used as steps, and paved the terrace with more natural stone, randomly placed and interplanted with white creeping thyme. Then she found a huge old stone jar ("strong enough, I thought, to stand up to the building"), which she and the artist together placed at one end of the terrace, its lid lying on the ground beside it as though it had slipped off. The jar holds water and one or two water lilies. With no other plants and no furnishings, the space is suitably spare and striking.

I was not surprised to hear, however, that there are plans for a vegetable and herb garden—the artist is a superb cook—surrounded by an orchard. And, on a recent visit, Nancy brought a bouquet of outrageous dahlias the size of butter dishes—some striped, others tightly-furled, in deep shades of garnet and crimson—to tempt her client. She had grown them from tubers carried home from a dahlia-finding expedition to Oregon and Washington.

"Details take a lot of energy," Nancy admitted. "It's how you see things. Some people are just interested in the big picture. You do the details for people who understand."

LEFT: *Nancy's whimsical structures, offering shelter for birds and small dogs, or rest for the gardener, are often placed at the end of a path or axis, to catch and please your eye.*
BELOW: *A large stone water vessel was found to ornament the stone terrace Nancy created outside a contemporary artist's studio in Sharon, Connecticut. The scale and simplicity of the jar appealed to both artist and designer.*

Piet Oudolf

THE COUNTRYSIDE OF HOLLAND, where Piet Oudolf lives, has the same serenely picturesque look today that Rembrandt captured in his etchings three hundred years ago. The land is astonishingly flat, sliced by rivers and canals, and is often blanketed with mist, through which rows of poplar trees, slowly moving figures of grazing cows, warm-toned farmhouses, and the occasional windmill materialize against the horizon.

Everywhere there are gardens. The softness of the climate (except for the wind), the fertile ground, and a plenitude of water have resulted in a proliferation of flowers in every backyard. When the Dutch are not out bicycling on the country roads, they are surely gardening. And they have the good fortune to be within driving distance—everything in this small country is within one day's drive—of the extraordinary selection of perennials for sale at Piet Oudolf's nursery and home. Not only can the Dutch gardener buy unusual hardy perennials there, many of them improved cultivars of America's native meadow flowers, but he or she can come home with refreshing new ideas about how best to combine those perennials. Piet's nursery catalog is full of helpful suggestions about what plants complement each other, and his sales beds are set up to reinforce those suggestions, clustering together plants that Piet feels would make "good neighbors." Customers can also learn by example, walking around the splendid front and back gardens that extend out from Piet's house and around his nursery.

Piet is, foremost, a brilliant designer of gardens. He is a master of the new wave of Dutch and German

PRECEDING PAGES: *An overview of the front garden at Piet Oudolf's home and nursery in Holland shows the powerful, yet playful, green architecture he uses to set off his bold, naturalistic sweeps of plants.* LEFT: *Piet values the autumn seedheads and silhouettes of his perennials as much as the flowers.* BELOW: *A view looking into the front garden.* RIGHT: *Angelica gigas, in tight bud, and stalks of knotweed rise above sedums of similar coloring in one of Piet's lush August borders.*

gardening, in which perennials, especially those with a natural air, are prized as much for their structure as for their flowers and are massed in luxuriant combinations of textures and shapes. His gardens are as stunning in fall and winter as they are lavish in summer, with seed heads, stalks, and dried inflorescences sometimes creating even more striking pictures than the flowers and leaves that preceded them. His designs, Piet says, are inspired by nature, and he favors perennials that have a natural look to them, often using meadow plants and grasses as main characters in his borders. Piet is one of the many Europeans who valued our American meadow flowers when we were still taking them for granted. Asters, eupatoriums, bee balms, veronicastrums, knotweeds, filipendulas, and goldenrods, all denizens of our eastern fields, are used again and again as the backbone of his gardens. But Piet grounds his naturalistic gardens with stout evergreen topiary and densely clipped hedges, playing this static green architecture against the wildness of his borders.

ABOVE: *Pear trees clipped into rectangular columns and a rolling serpent of a beech hedge give dramatic structure to Piet's nursery.* **RIGHT**: *Piet's wife, Anja, helps run the nursery in back of their farmhouse. Perennials and grasses are displayed in groupings to suggest combinations Piet thinks are most effective in the garden.*

The first sight one has when approaching Piet Oudolf's farmhouse, on a country road outside the town of Hummelo, is of red roofs and a huge dark green rolling serpent of a hedge that extends out from the farm buildings into the countryside. Piet calls this undulating stretch of clipped beech, which shields his nursery from view, his dragon hedge, and laughingly wonders what his neighbors thought when he first shaped it into what now appears to be an amazing apparition in the misted pastureland. Within this rollercoaster hedge, rows and rows of perennials are displayed for sale, and long beds are artistically planted in combinations Piet finds pleasing. In the back of his catalog, he lists each plant he sells and then suggests four or five plants he thinks would combine well with it. (This is what Piet calls his Good Neighbors list.) The nursery area is contained by the hedge and farm buildings, and is an area both functional and practical, but it is surrounded by a dazzling display of flowers, blooming in such profusion that they seem to have escaped the confines of the nursery beds. (In early July, for example, you walk down the rows through a haze of blue caused by breathtaking masses of campanulas and delphiniums.) The lushness of the nursery garden is punctuated by a series of tall columns of trained and clipped pear trees. Piet's wife, Anja, now runs the business of the nursery to afford Piet more time for designing gardens.

An example of his talents is found at the front of their house, where he has laid out a dramatic and complex garden. At first glance, the design of the garden looks traditionally formal. A brick path runs down a central axis, ending at a fat clump of hydrangea plant-

ed in front of a tall beech hedge. More hedges, like a series of curtains on either side of the main path, open to reveal gorgeous masses of perennials. But as you stand there, you soon realize that everything is slightly off kilter—on purpose, of course. The central brick path is interrupted several times by circular beds filled with *Hosta sieboldiana* and wild ginger—except that the beds are not really circles but ovals laid on an angle across the path. Side paths go off at odd angles too, and the more you look the more you see that there is a subtle asymmetry to all the structural details. The hedges themselves, used as a series of backdrops, are not always clipped in a severe geometric line but often rise and dip in waves above the flowers or lean sharply toward the center of the garden.

The flower beds wave in and out as they extend down the sides of the garden, with the result that you can't see everything at once, and you must strike off onto

the lawn and weave in through the curved, disappearing inner paths to capture the ever-changing spectacle of Piet's perennials. Nothing is staked; everything is allowed to move with the wind and stand up on its own, as it would in nature. Tall plants are often frankly placed up front, especially see-through ones like the ornamental grass stipa, or the slender knotweed *Persicaria amplexicaule*. Everywhere, it seems, Piet is breaking the rules.

Even Piet's use of color is cheerfully audacious, with dashes of orange and red, or bold blocks of yellow, enlivening his predominant schemes of purple, lavender, magenta, mauve, and white. He combines colors with flair and sensitivity, knowing just when to throw in buttons of deep red (knautia) among spires of buff yellow (*Digitalis ferruginea*), or interweave discs of orange (*Achillea* 'Terracotta') with pea flowers of pale blue (a beautiful form of galega called 'Lady Wilson') to bring the flowers to life. In one electric patch of

LEFT: *The central axis of Piet's garden is interrupted by oval beds of plants, set asymmetrically into the lawn and surrounded by uneven swirls of brick. Fat columns of yew seem almost to have been dropped haphazardly into the garden, adding weight to Piet's display of perennials. Hostas in the foreground are newly underplanted with European ginger.*
ABOVE: *A series of yew and beech hedges, clipped in a combination of waves and lines, serves as a theatrical backdrop to Piet's flower garden.*

border, Piet mingles a striking red yarrow (*Achillea* 'Feurland') with purple spikes of *Salvia superba*, then adds bladder campion with its fragile white cuplike flowers, along with shaggy heads of scarlet bee balm. But, as sparkling as these color combinations are, it is the contrasting structures of the plants, you realize, that really make their pairings so effective. Piet says that height and color do not matter in a garden. What he means, I think, is that the traditional ways of using height and color no longer matter—and that structure and pattern matter so much more.

Piet successfully illustrates in his garden that there are no unbreakable rules when it comes to arranging borders of plants; that sometimes the tallest plants are best in the front, for a sense of drama, and the ground-hugging ones can belong in the back, for early spring interest; that a formal garden does not have to be symmetrical, it just has to "feel" right; and that the archi-

tecture, the composition of the plants, is the most crucial element. Besides relying on perennials that have bold or interesting shapes, Piet adds some solid green topiary to contrast with his flowers and grasses, giving added weight to his design. Fat, solitary columns of yew march down either side of the central axis of his front garden, not in any obvious, ordered way—some are placed on the lawn, others right in the garden beds—but always serving to balance and ground the more ephemeral groupings of flowering plants.

"It is very easy to get a garden out of balance," Piet remarked, as he walked with a critical, caring eye along his borders. This can happen as a garden matures, as it is "let go" to some degree, and as the more invasive plants overpower others that are more delicate, thus changing the dynamics of the border. And it is why a certain amount of static structure, whether in the form of hardscaping or green architecture, helps maintain a balanced picture.

Piet was trained as an architect before he became a plantsman and designer of gardens, which explains some of his concentration on forms within the garden space. But his passion is plants, perennials and grasses in particular, and it is his great feel for bringing together their differing characters, for getting the most out of their interaction, that makes his gardens uniquely spe-

LEFT: *Piet's flower borders weave in and out along the sides of his garden in such a way that all is not revealed at once. The seedheads of alliums wave with grasses in front of a late summer display of filipendulas and Joe-Pye weed.*
RIGHT: *Piet often uses tall plants up front in his borders. His preference is for perennials with a natural grace and wild air. The height and color of the plants, he says, do not really matter.*

cial. He uses many rare and unusual forms of perennials, some of which he has introduced into commerce himself. We are beginning to find his plants in American nurseries, new cultivars with better habit and longer bloom, like *Gaura* 'Whirling Butterflies', *Monarda* 'Scorpio,' and *Salvia verticillata* 'Purple Rain.' It was in frustration that he started to propagate and hybridize his own plants, after he was unable to find the cultivars he wanted in any quantity for his designs. Piet's gardens, no matter how small, always have a lavishness that requires a generous massing of plants.

A small garden Piet designed in southern Holland illustrates the luxuriousness of his planting, even in a

LEFT: *A knotweed,* Polygonum amplexicaule, *blooms wildly with crimson spires behind a tripod. The knotweeds are one of Piet's favorite plant families.* RIGHT: *Piet has underplanted a large cherry tree in his garden with a circle of the striking* Euphorbia wulfenii. BELOW: *The plants Piet combines with grasses, he feels, should be "nature-like." There are almost no variegated plants in Piet's gardens—too artificial, he says. He favors meadow plants like eupatoriums, burnets, knotweeds, thalictrums, astrantias, and filipendulas.*

TOP and BOTTOM LEFT: *For clients in southern Holland, Piet filled a small suburban plot with lush plantings of shrubs and perennials to achieve the jungle-like feeling they sought. Stands of bamboo and ornamental grasses are mixed with ferny-leaved* Selinum tenuifolium, *tall thalictrums, knotweeds, coneflowers, and astrantias.* RIGHT: *At a larger garden in De Heurne, Piet combined topiary near the house with lavish mixed borders around the lawn.*

confined space. The owners wanted a "jungle effect" in their garden, which extended out from their low modern house and deck. Piet filled the entire backyard, perhaps a quarter acre in size and bounded closely by neighbors, with a lush, robust mixture of perennials, shrubs, and trees through which narrow winding paths disappear and then reappear only to curve out of view in another direction. The plants he chose are ones that have a natural air, cultivars of plants you might find in meadows and light woodland, and the result is a wild feeling to the garden, almost as though it had occurred naturally. As you walk through it, you become lost in its textures and shapes, completely forgetting that this magical piece of land is no more than a modest rectangular suburban lot. Piet speaks often of the atmosphere of a garden, the feeling of the place he hopes to create with his plants. Here, in this small yet profuse garden, standing among towering bamboos and lace-topped meadow rues, he seems as pleased with the result as his clients. He called the garden "a translation of their wishes with my plants."

The jungle-woodland feeling of this garden might seem unremarkable in my home territory of the northeastern United States, where the natural understory of our second-growth woods and meadow edges has the

same sort of atmosphere, and where we often hack away jungly growth to build our gardens. But in the open country of the Netherlands, a land without forests, the sense of losing oneself within a natural-seeming tangle of leaves, flowers, and dappled sunlight is quite extraordinary. Except for a clipped beech hedge that curves around a path near the front of the house, no evergreen structure interrupts the wildness of this modernistic garden. But this is a departure for Piet, for he invariably incorporates bold topiary in his garden designs. Topiary is, after all, part of his garden heritage, so splendidly illustrated at William and Mary's former palace, Het Loo,

near Piet's home, where the hedges, parterres, tunnels, and topiary have been magnificently restored.

At a garden in De Heurne, close to the border of Germany, Piet has created a theatrical contrast between mannered, controlled topiary and loosely luxurious beds of perennials and shrubs. A formal parterred garden of hybrid tea roses existed just outside the doors of the house when Piet was hired by the residents to redesign the property. He pulled out the roses, which were diseased (and so ugly in winter), and filled the low boxwood parterres with yew—not with tulips or annuals or colored pebbles, but with yew! What a bizarre,

dramatic idea! The clipped yew, which is a darker green and rougher texture than the box, rises just a few inches above its boxwood girdle in most cases (in some instances it is sculpted into tall pillars and plump mounds), and the subtle play of texture and color between these two evergreens gives this very traditional patterned garden a strong modern flip. Introducing a third texture of green, Piet surrounded the parterre garden with a clipped beech hedge, which encloses it and makes it serenely private.

Arched openings in the hedge give a teasing glimpse of wild color and lushly disparate foliage beyond this quiet world of green architecture. As you walk through the hedge, you find yourself on a sunny lawn that swims past huge, curving borders of flowers massed in sumptuous profusion. Shrub roses mingle with vast sweeps of perennials—campanulas, cranesbills, phlox, filipendulas, veronicas. Explosions of grasses and carpets of herbs weave through the borders, and feathery annual herbs, like dill and fennel, seed themselves along the edges.

The contrast between the two parts of the garden underlines the power of each. Without the flower borders, the parterre garden might seem too severe, too monochromatic and unchanging. And without the restorative calm of the green topiary, one might become sated with the extravagance of color, fragrance, texture, and shape in the overscaled, romantically overblown flower garden.

Piet has made certain that, here, too, there will be beauty in fall and winter as well as in spring and summer. From the strong architecture of the evergreen parterres, perhaps at its most stunning in winter, you walk during that season into a flower garden still full of interest, a garden of parchment colors, of arching grasses, pale plumes and tawny seed heads, of rustling leaves and rosy berries and hips.

Nothing in Piet's borders is cut down until spring, and, I suspect, it is in late fall and winter, without all the fanfare of flower color, that his gardens seem most natural to him. To reflect images of a wild landscape in his gardens is Piet's goal. He speaks of his preference for plants with "natural charm" (you do not often find variegated plants in his gardens—"too artificial"), and of his desire to make his borders of perennials and grasses "give you the feeling you are walking in nature." And yet Piet does not forsake the traditions of his country altogether. He marries this new naturalistic style of planting with offbeat evergreen geometry, grounding his wildly sumptuous perennials with sweeping lines of hedges and bold exclamations of topiary.

PRECEDING PAGES: Piet filled box parterres with yew, clipped just three inches higher and subtly contrasting with the boxwood in texture and color. Occasional mounds and pillars of yew rise out of the parterres. ABOVE: The sumptuous borders on the other side of the beech hedge contrast romantically with the dramatic severity of the topiary garden.

Louis Benech

Louis Bench

WALKING DOWN ONE OF THE ALLÉES of horse chestnuts in the Tuileries on a brilliantly sunny day, Louis Benech conjectured about what its designer, André Le Nôtre, would do to this grand Parisian garden in front of the Louvre if he were alive today. Louis feels certain he would change the Tuileries to fit the times while preserving the natural order, balance, and grand simplicity of his seventeenth-century design.

But it is Louis, collaborating with fellow designer Pascal Cribier, who has been responsible for adapting

the Tuileries for the twentieth and twenty-first centuries. "I don't like gardens that are signed and dated historically," he says.

Gardens, he believes, should evolve with the times, suit their present-day function, and fit the capabilities of the people who use them. "The evolution of gardens is really a matter of economics," Louis explained. The reason our gardens are becoming more and more natural is that informality is more economical, involving less labor. With considerably less money to spend and a dearth of willing laborers, we are not tempted to design gardens on a magnificent scale. Instead of gardens to impress, grand settings for royalty—Le Nôtre's mandate in Louis XIV's day—we need humanized, simplified parks and gardens that nurture, embrace, and solace us.

With this in mind, Louis and Pascal have shrunk the great, dazzling paths of white sand at the Tuileries, and added more grass. This they have graded into softly curving "cushions," or mounds. By mounding the lawns, a greater expanse of green meets the eye; in effect, Louis explains, "the pillowed lawns eat the mineral aspect" of the garden. The sixteen small squares that lead off the broad central axis have been restored, and the parterres in the sun-flooded great lawn just below the Louvre now sway with an unpretentious, light-hearted mixture of perennials and annuals in cheerful shades of pink, blue, and white.

As we walked in the filtered light of the central *allée*, looking into the shadowy squares on our left and right, Louis talked about his impressions of the Tuileries. "I feel this place is tiny, even though it is quite large." It is the compartments of grass, water, and trees, and the sense of enclosure they create, that give this great public park its feeling of intimacy. Louis's grandparents lived next to the Tuileries when he was a child and he remembers playing here in the white sand paths. "As a boy, I didn't think of it as a garden, because it was full of sand. A garden is a green place, not a white place." With the lawns regraded and extended today, and with the trees and topiary replanted, there is more greenery to contrast with the broad sand *allées,* and endless places to sit in sun or shade. Parisians as well as tourists rendezvous in the garden, drawing up chairs to sunbathe by the circular fountains, or to cool themselves in the dappled shade of the squares.

Louis was responsible for the new planting schemes at the Tuileries. "I was a gardener; I knew plants," he says with disarming simplicity. Indeed, he started as a gardener in the 1980s, working for a wealthy property owner in the French countryside. At one point, his employer offered him more money for the work he was doing, and Louis turned it down, asking instead for the freedom to design the garden. "Allow me to fly as a butterfly," he proposed, with all the charm of a Frenchman. His client readily agreed, and Louis's career as a garden designer was launched. Louis had trained first at Hilliers Nursery in England, and there became a dedicated plantsman. He speaks with a certain envy about the wealth of plants in England, coveting their accessiblity. The French, he says, unlike the English, are more interested in the design of a garden than in the individual plants, and consequently there is not the same demand for an interesting selection of cultivars in his country.

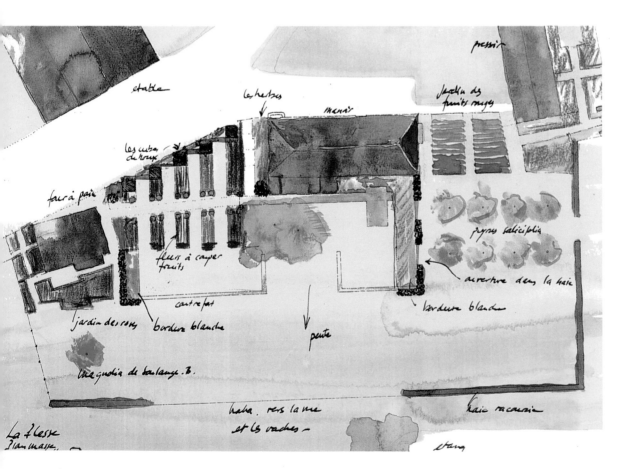

LEFT: *The garden of cutting flowers and vegetables (typical of Normandy) becomes a liaison between the main house and a timbered bread oven pavilion on the left.* **RIGHT:** *Louis terraced the sloping land in front of the house with stone walls, plumping the lawns like pillows to echo the rolling pastures.*

180 *Rethinking the French Formal Garden*

With his love of plants, Louis adds a rich and charming floriferousness to his classically inspired French gardens. While he uses strong geometry and spacial balance based on the French formal tradition, he breaks any stiffness by giving his designs a very natural air, bowing, he would say, to the economies of our times. "Gardening is always artificial," he says, "but now we are working with a more natural spirit." The gardens are easier to maintain and to restore. "I believe in working with who the people are and what they need," he says, and thus he makes his gardens appropriate to the owners' lifestyles and the settings in which they live.

In a garden in Normandy that Louis considers a favorite among his projects, his design was influenced by the atmosphere of the site as well as by the character of the buildings and the owner's desires. Called La Plesse, the fifteenth-century manor house nestles among striped stucco-and-timber farm buildings—stables, a cow barn, a house for the bread oven—in lush, rolling pastureland dotted with cows and fruit trees. From every aspect of the house and garden, this verdant, picturesque, homely landscape dominates the view. The owner, a passionate gardener, gave Louis free rein to design a garden that suited the place.

Louis wanted the boundaries of his garden to be transparent enough to embrace views of the hilly countryside. From the back of the house, steps lead down a lawn that dips between two terraced gardens to a mown field below it. The field is bounded on the right and left by the wings of a formally clipped yew hedge that stop abruptly, and suprisingly, on either side of a long center swath of mown grass, allowing a generous unobstructed view of the pond and pastures beyond. To create an invisible boundary, Louis constructed a ha-ha (a stone-walled ditch) to extend along this large

gap in the hedging, which prevents the cows from getting into the garden but does not interrupt the view. The two wings of broken hedge give the impression of a frame, offering a suggestion of formality. Thus Louis merely hints at classical geometric structure.

Just outside the house, on either side of the descending sweep of lawn, Louis leveled the grade with retaining walls of stucco and stone in order to hold two small flower gardens. He then mounded the leveled ground of the garden areas as though they were softly plumped pillows, echoing the rounded pastures in the distance. On one side, a tall yew hedge extends out from the house to the retaining wall and serves as a background for a romantic mixed border of white flowers. On the other side, the striped wall of a timbered, stuccoed shed (the pavilion for the bread oven), catty-cornered to the house, is the background for a *potager*. Here, narrow rows of flowers repeat the stripes of the shed and are intersected by a center grass panel, bordered by a succession of small box bushes,

that leads toward the house lawn and the white garden opposite. The long thin beds, divided by grass paths and billowing with flowers—red dahlias, lavender lupines, blue erigerons, pink roses—in simple groupings, slope gently toward the view, ending with espaliered pear trees and apples trained like goblets through which you see the distant pastures.

"I didn't want to touch the landscape," Louis said about designing this charming garden. With his soft, rounded shapes of lawn, flowers, and bushes, he echoes the hills, and with the trees and bold, interrupted hedging, he frames the pastoral scenery. "It is a place I like very much because it's simple," he said. Perhaps the unpretentiousness of the place strikes a chord in Louis because he himself is so modest and unassuming, and because he feels it is appropriate and of our time.

I drove one day with Louis to another property in the rural countryside near Versailles, where he is adding new garden sections and rooms to a very elaborately structured and well-established chateau garden.

He was quick to tell me this was not typical of his work, speaking, I think, of the grandness of the garden, and referring to the fact that most of its architectural green structure—magnificent hedges and topiary—was in place long before he became involved with the garden's design. Much of his work there entails improving the existing gardens as well as adding new ones.

Louis had recently replanted the existing double flower border with lushly textured perennials and purple-leaved shrubs in sumptuous combinations. In addition, he had nurtured a meadow dappled with wildflowers, created a small white garden patterned with hedges, trees, and flowers, and was concentrating his efforts on a whimsical folly of a garden at one end of the moat that cuts a wide ribbon of water along the front of the chateau. That this garden was being built for the particular enjoyment of the resident geese and ducks seemed remarkable to no one involved, least of all Louis. At the edge of the water, he constructed a broad landing out of wood, which he carpeted with grass. He then ran a path

from the landing up a bank through plantings of lythrum and flag iris (both happy to grow in wet ground) to a fanciful igloo-shaped gazebo made of teak and leafing willow branches, where the waterfowl can enjoy some shade. Two enormous jardinieres are positioned on either side of the gazebo, from which water can spill (to the delight of the ducks) back into the moat. Making this "beach," as Louis calls it, for the ducks and geese required a creative attitude, something Louis obviously delights in.

The white garden, extending out from a terrace of the chateau, is Louis's brilliant expression of "something formal but modern." A Calder statue dances on the central rectangular lawn in front of a grid of white poplars. Beyond, clipped hedges of variegated red-stemmed dogwood (*Cornus alba* 'Elegantissima') jut out into the central axis of lawn in a startling series of rows, and are interplanted with hydrangeas and white Japanese anemones. Two small rooms on either side of the lawn are enclosed by hedges of an uncommon and very beautiful variegated winter-flowering dogwood,

PRECEDING PAGES: *"I didn't want to touch the landscape,"* Louis says of designing this Normandy garden. LEFT: *A broken line of yew and an invisible ha-ha, or walled ditch, end the garden but allow views of picturesque farmland beyond.* RIGHT: *Sweet rocket, rue, delphinium, and clematis adorn a mixed border of white flowers just outside the fifteenth-century manor house. Louis invariably graces his formal gardens with a profusion of unpretentious flowers.*

ABOVE: *Sharply clipped hedges of variegated cornelian cherry* (Cornus mas 'Variegata') *and inky green yew play with light and dark in a formal white garden near Versailles.* BELOW: *In this same garden, a dramatic series of hedged enclosures of variegated dogwood* (Cornus alba 'Elegantissima') *are filled with aruncus and white Siberian iris in spring, and hydrangeas and white-flowering Japanese anemones in late summer.* RIGHT: *A Calder sculpture interrupts the main axis of the white garden framed by a line of shimmering white poplars.*

Cornus mas 'Variegata.' One room Louis has filled with flowers—roses and white-flowering annuals; the other room, serving as an antechamber to a lane leading to the tennis court, is empty except for a pattern of different types of pear trees.

For the same clients, Louis was asked to design a Mediterranean garden in Saint Tropez. Louis feels that

this garden, called Font Vert, or Green Fountain, is especially well suited to the owners and to the place. "I try to work in different ways in different places," he says, always stressing the importance of the site and the owners' needs. At Font Vert, Louis worked with many of Le Nôtre's precepts, but on a more modest scale. He first concentrated on grading levels, flattening a slope

into a series of terraces below the house. He took down evergreen trees to widen the space in front of the house, making the garden "more simple" and creating a strong main axis. This now leads your eye down a broad lawn to an ornamental pool and beyond to a view of a church steeple and the blue Mediterranean sea. A swimming pool at the opposite end of the axis, behind the house,

LEFT: *In a garden in Saint Tropez, Louis planted herbs in rows above a central panel of lawn, repeating the lines of a vineyard in the distance.* **TOP RIGHT:** *Lavender, interplanted with Russian sage (Perovskia), border a walk beyond the patio of the house.* **BOTTOM RIGHT:** *A field of rosemary, clipped in diagonal lines, flourishes between the lavender walk and an orchard of ancient olive trees Louis had brought to the site.*

is partially concealed by the wings of a yew hedge, "so you don't know where the pool starts and finishes," but you can just catch the shimmer of water as you look out beyond to the vineyards in the distance. The client was hesitant about the hedge when Louis proposed it, so Louis first planted maize to simulate the hedge, thus convincing his client of its effectiveness.

On a series of terraces above the main garden axis, Louis planted Mediterranean natives in striking grid-like patterns. On the top level, ancient olive trees were planted in tall grass and underplanted with woad and California poppies. Below them, clipped rosemary was laid out in rows to match the lines of a vineyard glimpsed in a field beyond. Just above the main lawn, Louis created a walk through hazy blue rows of lavender. When first planning the garden, he used stakes to help his eye connect things, to get the correct scale and balance in his design. "Balance does not necessarily mean symmetry, which can be boring," Louis points out. "There are plans and then there is what you see," he says with a touch of irony, knowing from experience that the end result in a garden rarely jibes with its design on paper.

The overall look of his Mediterranean garden is frankly geometric in style, and yet, as in many of Louis's gardens, it is softened by distinctive plantings of flow-ers. The spare, rectangular pool, for example, is felicitously embroidered around its edges with the starburst heads of white-flowering agapanthus, which multiply with their reflection in the water. The five-hundred-year-old olives stand in a brilliant mille-fleur tapestry of gold, orange, and pale yellow woven from poppies and woad. The severe rows of lavender are interrupted by hazy explosions of Russian sage. Although the geometric terraces and broad main axis here are in the classical French tradition, imposing regularity on an irregular site, Louis's introduction of a diversity of plants, his lightness of style, and modern sensibility update this tradition.

In a garden in Sologne, where many French people go in the autumn for hunting season, Louis devised a modern formal garden to be at its best in the fall. The principle of his design was to keep the garden as uncomplicated as possible, using strong groupings of plants that would be easy to maintain. The various buildings of the hunting lodge were connected by hedges, thus creating an inner yard (originally graveled and used for parking cars), which Louis then planted with grass and bordered with a frame of native heather (*Calluna vulgaris*). This heather grows naturally all through the adjacent woods, but here Louis planted it

PRECEDING PAGES: *The flower heads of white agapanthus dance around a pool below the center lawn in the Saint Tropez garden. Louis underplanted the agapanthus with cape myrtle (*Myrsine africana). TOP LEFT: *Spare geometric panels of heather and a viburnum hedge ornament a hunting lodge in Sologne where Louis was asked to design a garden that would be easy to maintain.* BOTTOM LEFT: *Dogwoods were added to the woods surrounding the garden.* RIGHT: *Louis planted the native heather (*Calluna vulgaris) *like a carpet, framing a simple lawn and connecting the various buildings at the lodge.*

in bold geometric blocks that "can be mowed as flat as the grass." Behind the heather, he designed verdant borders of low shrubs that have a good autumn display of flowers, fruit, and tinted foliage. This is, simply, the garden proper. Beyond its confines, the clients just wanted to enjoy views of the countryside. Louis laced the natural woodland with colonies of dogwoods and, in an adjoining field, planted an orchard of cherry trees. The garden remains easy to maintain, but now has the color, patterns, and textures of Louis's unpretentiously bold plantings.

Although his gardens always relate to the landscape and the house near which they are located—and, at the same time, reflect his inclination toward a modern formality in design—Louis's love of plants and his discerning use of them bring a liveliness and pure charm to the sophistication of his garden schemes.

"I love gardens that keep a sense of purpose," Louis says. "What I hate today in gardens is people doing things without any purpose, without connection to the place, to the owners, to the garden's function. I don't consider a garden art," he went on to say. "It is unsaleable. A Cubist garden, for instance, is nonsense. I don't see the point of it." A garden, Louis feels, is not shaped so much by new ideas as it is by economic situations. "You should be able to date a garden as belonging to a particular time."

The desire for low maintenance due to a lack of labor and time must then dictate the designs of our modern gardens. Therefore, they are smaller, simpler, more down-to-earth, more natural. And that suits Louis just fine.

Afterword

WHEN ERICA FIRST APPROACHED ME about writing this book, I thought, yes, it's time I dusted the dirt off my knees, time I went to see other gardeners and learned of other visions. What fun, I thought, how broadening, to become familiar with new places and absorb new ideas. I was aware, too, that sometimes it takes getting out of your own backyard and seeing gardens elsewhere to enable you to reevaluate your garden, to take a fresh critical look at your own efforts.

And that is exactly what happened. After traveling across the United States and Europe—talking with the designers, seeing their gardens, witnessing the care and attention to detail that went into their designs—I was struck with what was lacking in mine.

Why, for example, didn't I have any water in my garden? Steve Martino would not dream of designing a garden in which water was not a central feature, knowing how essential its cooling, soothing character is in a hot climate. Madison Cox speaks again and again about the magic created by the sound of water in a garden—revered, he points out, in the Mogul gardens of India and in Italian gardens. In the smallest city space, he finds room for a dripping fountain, and centers his garden around it. Nancy McCabe shows in her own country garden how easy it is to add water, merely placing a stone trough full of water in a flower bed, or siting one against a house wall, and recirculating the water it holds through a simple spout above it. A pot of flowering jasmine set casually to one side on the shelf of the trough lightens and dresses its sturdy plainness there, creating a picture that delights the eye as well as the ear.

With my tail between my legs, I returned home dissatisfied, shocked, that I could have been content for so many years without water in my garden. I prowled around for likely spots to introduce some. The curved stone wall outside my bathroom window would do nicely for a modest fountain—a small stone creature, perhaps, spouting water into a shallow basin in the gravel below. And where could I place a simple rectangular pool to reflect the sky? One would be lovely along my woodland path among snowdrops, hellebores, and ferns (a garden area more beautiful in my mind's eye than in reality, riddled by midsummer with clumps of Japanese knotweed, rampant poison ivy, and thickets of brambles).

I realized that my garden might benefit from other aspects of the designers' work and visions as well. Consider Patrick Chassé's concern with the surrounding environment, how he is always talking about the edges of a garden and how important it is to make the transition from garden to natural landscape by planting natives along those edges. Why hadn't I done this? I WILL do this! I will plant as many bushes of winterberry as I can afford, and also the native gray panicled dogwood (*Cornus racemosa*) in colonies along the edges

LEFT: *Appearing as a grace note, a mullein flowers where it seeded in the path to my small vegetable garden. I enjoy a little wildness within the hedged strictures of my garden.* RIGHT: *Crab apples line the walk to the house, recalling the apple orchards that were once a vital aspect of our town.*

of my property. These two indigenous shrubs are a part of the natural transition in my countryside between woods and fields. I will add the fall-flowering witch hazel, shad, and summersweet (*Clethra alnifolia*) beneath the maples and ash trees that bound my garden, for these are typical understory shrubs in the surrounding landscape.

From Piet Oudolf's example, I was convinced not to cut down all my perennials in the winter. When Piet plants a garden, he thinks as much about how it will look in late fall and winter as it will in spring and summer, and he chooses perennials for their silhouettes and seed heads as much as for their flowers. Why do I cut down everything in the name of neatness? Surely, I thought, looking at the bleakness of my winter beds, the bowed spears of Siberian iris, the blackened heads of rudbeckias, and the bleached puffs of asters are more pleasing to see from November to March than bare earth and truncated stalks.

Alain David Idoux showed me how the simplest stones could become sculptured features at the end of an axis. He taught me how satisfying it is to create something from what is at hand, to experiment with land art. I will look now at my weathered lichen-mottled stones, tumbled down and scattered from the farm walls of the last century, in a new light, as possible sculptures to site in my garden at the end of a path or beneath a tree.

I returned from visiting Dan Pearson and Nancy Power resolved to be bolder and wilder with color and masses of plants in my garden. I want now to play more with my palette, throw in more red, more orange—to excite things more. And I want to plant in bigger waves, grouping ten or twenty of one perennial, not a niggling two or three; clustering generous groups of one shrub, not dotting one here and one there.

LEFT: *Leeks seem appropriate plants for my farmhouse garden, but rather than pull the bulbs for the kitchen, I let them flower. Beyond the herb garden hedges, I will plant native shad and summersweet— bleeding the edges of my garden into the natural landscape, as Patrick Chassé would do.*

After seeing Nancy McCabe's charming designs for chairs and tables, and the simple café chairs and iron tables fashioned by Alain Idoux for eating alfresco in Provence, I came home horrified to think how I've lived for years virtually oblivious to the miserable appearance of my terrace furniture. How could I have tolerated those mildewed, glaring white, plastic-webbed chairs and table all this time? Well, yes, they are lightweight and easy to move around, and I'll admit they're comfortable. But what an offense to the eye! I realize now that a garden's furnishings are part of the whole picture. They add to the atmosphere of the place, and their selection needs as much thought as the plants we put into our garden beds.

I came back thinking about the meaning of a garden, asking myself if my garden relates to my house and the surrounding landscape in a symbolic way. I had watched Alain Idoux plant a spiral of almond trees in one garden to answer the curve of the mountains in the distance. Louis Benech rounded a lawn like a pillow to echo the rolling pastures just beyond his garden. Ron Lutsko planted humps of golden grasses to repeat the tawny hills. His strict lines of lavender in one garden were meant to recall the orchards that once patterned the adjacent countryside.

Did my garden show a sense of place, was its atmosphere right? It is a New England sort of garden, meant to suit the prim, unpretentious nineteenth-century

LEFT: *The view across the main flower garden, framed in privet, to narrow borders along a hemlock hedge. I would like to find or fashion a more original stone object or sculpture for the end of this axis.*
BELOW: *Spurred on by the examples of Alain Idoux and Nancy McCabe, I am rethinking my garden furniture. Here, an uninspired teak bench from a catalog has weathered to acceptability under a listing arbor in the herb garden.*

farmhouse it surrounds. The property is set in a quiet river valley once bustling with produce from apple orchards and dairy cows. The view from its flower beds is of rolling hillsides quilted with the pattern of stone-walled pastures and meadows. Patches of second-growth woodland edging the fields are still sectioned by crumbling farm walls and lines of mossy, silver-barked apple trees.

I realized that my original inclination to create a garden of old-fashioned sweet-scented perennials, shrubs, and trees—peonies, lilacs, crab apples, old roses, mock orange, daffodils, lilies, asters, and herbs—in a series of simple geometric enclosures was appropriately reminiscent of the countryside and its old architecture. A certain wildness and unkemptness that I've allowed within the hedged strictures of my garden echoes the haphaz-

ard lushness of the parceled meadows and the richly littered understory of the woods.

I knew I should stick to a certain plainness in my garden, that I should resist the temptation to plant cannas and banana plants—in fact, I should resist all the exotic plants that are so chic now and so excitingly used in our most forward-thinking gardens. Instead, my goal will be to grow more natives, concentrate on fragrance (often bred out of our most modern hybrids), and adhere to an unstudied chasteness in the choice of my plants. For in the end what I want is what our ten designers strive to capture in their garden designs: a sympathetic atmosphere and a deeply felt, satisfying sense of place.

Mulleins seed with abandon in my garden. I love their straightforward yellow and white verticals shooting up in unexpected places, as they do here—a nice contrast to feverfew—along the walk from the kitchen terrace to the barn.

Acknowledgments

WE WOULD LIKE ESPECIALLY TO THANK the ten designers who are featured in our book for the generous time they gave us, not only showing us their work, but thoughtfully, articulately explaining their vision. And we are exceedingly grateful to the garden owners who showed us the end results. Our thanks also go to the many friends and acquaintances who helped us develop the book, among them: Antonia Adezio, Rosie Atkins, Jennie Bernard, Edward Burlingame, Barbara Clark, Tania Compton, Laurie Frank, Paula Henderson, Karan Kapoor, Susan Kroeger, Elaine Lennard, Scott Stover, and Anne Wilson. Finally, we offer warm thanks to Jim Wageman for pulling the book together so beautifully, and to Leslie Stoker and Helen Pratt for their faith in us, which made *Breaking Ground* possible in the first place.

Designed by Jim Wageman, Wigwag

Typefaces used in this book are Sabon,
designed by Jan Tschichold, and Avenir,
designed by Adrian Frutiger

Printed and bound by Arnoldo Mondadori
Editore S.P.A., Verona, Italy